PARENTING AND TEACHING THE GIFTED

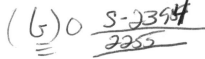

Rosemary Callard-Szulgit

Illustrations by Mark Szulgit

A SCARECROWEDUCATION BOOK

The Scarecrow Press, Inc.
Lanham, Maryland, and Oxford
2003

A SCARECROWEDUCATION BOOK

Published in the United States of America
by Scarecrow Press, Inc.
A Member of the Rowman & Littlefield Publishing Group
4720 Boston Way, Lanham, Maryland 20706
www.scarecroweducation.com

PO Box 317
Oxford
OX2 9RU, UK

British Library Cataloguing in Publication Information Available

Library of Congress Cataloging-in-Publication Data

Callard-Szulgit, Rosemary, 1946-
  Parenting and teaching the gifted / Rosemary Callard-Szulgit.
    p. cm.
  "A ScarecrowEducation book."
  Includes bibliographical references and index.
  ISBN 0-8108-4528-8 (alk. paper) — ISBN 0-8108-4529-6 (pbk. : alk. paper)
    1. Gifted children—Education. 2. Education—Parent participation. I. Title.

LC3993.2 .C35 2003
371.95—dc21

2002030577

♾️^{TM} The paper used in this publication meets the minimum requirements of
American National Standard for Information Sciences—Permanence of Paper
for Printed Library Materials, ANSI/NISO Z39.48-1992.
Manufactured in the United States of America.

First and foremost, to my mother, Josephine Eastman Stiles Callard. Mom was a woman decades of ahead of her time. She was brilliant, beautiful, very much a lady and always giving of herself to others, through life, church, her family, and community.

Dad, I've always admired you intelligence and down-to-earth approach, even if it wasn't my style. You kept me on firm ground.

Karl, my wonderful sweetheart, whose intelligence and magnanimous caring of friends and family I've always admired, along with children, Eric, Fern, and Mark, our family, who have taught me more about love and life.

Virginia, my very best friend.

My brothers, Dave and John, whom I love.

My friends, Jeanette and Pat, who, for as long as they each knew me, encouraged me to write the book they knew I had in me.

And Brenda, for typing. You are a sweetheart! Thank you.

CONTENTS

PREFACE

Writing this book has been a pleasure for me as a practical part of my thirty-four-year career in the public school and university settings, settings in which education for the gifted has been accepted/scorned, exemplified/vilified, and touted as elitist/integrated for students of all abilities. I have been able to help hundreds, if not thousands, of students and their parents understand and benefit from the strategies and programs available for gifted children, which work for all children. I've also helped dispel many of the myths associated with gifted children.

We know that differentiation is beneficial for all students, and that higher-level thinking skills are essential for everyone.

Synthesis, or creativity, is a joyful key in the learning process. Students thrive when making learning their own, displaying application projects with their very own creative touch.

Compacting can save weeks, months, and even years of repetitive work for gifted children.

Using an inclusive process, rather than an exclusive program, has become a much more healthy way to assimilate the education for our cognitively gifted children in today's schools, avoiding the labels of "you're gifted/you're not" and "you're in/you're out!" The dividing lines between the supposed "haves" and "have-nots" are being erased.

Yes, I do believe all children are gifted with individual and unique traits of their very own! However, we do have a cadre of children whose cognitive abilities far surpass those of their peers. Their knowledge base is far more expansive. To have these students study grade-level curricular areas they've already mastered, year after year after year, is unacceptable.

All children deserve to be educated at their levels of aptitude and accomplishment. *All!*

Teachers cannot do it alone. As the school day demands increased responsibilities in our ever-changing society, educators are desperately trying to service children with a multitude of thinking levels and emotional development in their classrooms. Parents can help. Administrators can help. District staff development coordinators can help by providing education in understanding the gifted and how to educate them, providing trainers in our school districts.

As a recovering perfectionist, I understand well the emotional pain that accompanies this dilemma for so many of our gifted children—their parents, too. We can provide counseling and many fine self-help books for these children to read and talk through with us.

Study skills and procrastination are not unique to just one or two achievement levels of children. Gifted children also need help in these arenas. Time management is becoming a necessity for our multipotential students, their parents, and other family members.

We can all help make this world a little better, as we help one another foster excellence and applicability in our schools throughout the country. My way of making this world a little better place in my lifetime is writing this book and supporting parents and teachers of gifted children, helping them realize the best education possible for their children.

Read, enjoy, and know I admire every single one of you parents and educators who are giving your best to this country's children—all of them.

INTRODUCTION

Parents of gifted children have often experienced the frustration of trying to get an appropriate education for their children in public and private schools.

Teachers of the gifted have equally experienced the frustration of trying to educate their gifted students while the requirements of special education, inclusion model, blending, and other classroom demands increasingly fragment their time and energies.

The information on parenting and teaching the gifted is presented through six main chapters. The format is question and answer, aimed at helping parents, teachers, and children find solutions to their queries through time-tested, applicable solutions.

These are the questions and answers for all who seek a fair and equitable education for the gifted. *Parenting and Teaching the Gifted* provides the solutions.

I

WHO ARE THE GIFTED
AND TALENTED?

Q. What exactly does being "gifted" mean?
A. By definition, the U.S. Department of Education reflects today's knowledge and thinking about gifted children (Ross 1993, 26):

> Children and youth with outstanding talent who perform or show the potential for performing at remarkably high levels of accomplishment when compared with others of their age, experience, or environment.
>
> These children and youth exhibit high-performance capability in intellectual, creative, and/or artistic areas, possess an unusual leadership capacity, or excel in specific academic fields. They require services or activities not ordinarily provided by the school.
>
> Outstanding talents are present in children and youth from all cultural groups, across all economic strata, and in all areas of human endeavor.

Whether you choose to support the use of this definition or not, the fact remains that hundreds and thousands of children in our schools have thinking and comprehension abilities that far surpass the norm of their peers.

Howard Gardner (1984) helped expand our understanding of human intelligence and gifts with his theory of the seven multiple intelligences:

Linguistic—verbal, reader, writer
Musical—melodic, learns through music
Logical/mathematical—strategist, conceptual, orderly
Spatial—imaging in pictures
Bodily kinesthetic—physical, athletic
Interpersonal—leader, understands people and their interactions
Intrapersonal—self-reflective

Unfortunately, many of our schools' gifted programs still focus just on the verbal/linguistic and logical/mathematical aspects of intelligence, a far cry from servicing the wealth of "gifts" and "learning styles" we've learned about through the research and understanding over the past two decades.

Q. Aren't all children gifted in some way, shape, or form?
A. Absolutely! Indeed, I do believe we all have our very own special gifts. I love my gift of red hair. I love my husband's gifts of genius, exceeding generosity, and gregariousness. I love my nephew's ability to think incredibly deep. In fact, every single student I've ever had throughout my thirty-four-year career possessed specific gifts.

I remember Sara with her most beautiful red curls and adorable freckles; Joe with his outrageous and wonderful gregariousness; Anne with her beautiful ballets steps; and Marie, with her loving sensitivity toward me when my mother passed away. I remember equally as well Christopher, who's now an honor student at Princeton; Chip, whose own three-year-old is exceeding bright; and Kelly, who is pursuing a dancing

career! These children and their specific gifts will always remain in my heart.

We do have children in our schools whose cognitive (thinking) abilities far surpass those of their peers (classmates), and we simply must serve these students educationally! This can be done through differentiation, compacting, independent study, and acceleration combined with enrichment.

Children who are capable of high performance, whose aptitude and abilities far exceed their peers, are gifted and need to be educated accordingly. This is where we need to combine enrichment with acceleration and differentiate our curriculums.

Q. Is stubbornness a predominant personality characteristic of highly gifted children?

A. This question brought an immense smile to my face, as I will always remember the comment my kindergarten teacher wrote to my parents on the first quarter report card going home:

"Rosemary is one of the most stubborn children I have ever had as a student!"

My parents' written reply was, "Yes, we know!"

Here I was, at the age of six, being "sold out" to the thinking and whims of the public school system! At least, that was my interpretation then.

Nothing was written about me testing eight years beyond my peers in reading nor being capable of doing math calculations equally as well! My teacher's primary concern was that I didn't/wouldn't always follow her instructions without questioning and/or offering alternatives. Of course, there are always two (or more) sides to every story, and it would be quite interesting to hear her side.

Now I'd like to think of myself as "assertive." Gifted children are often quite stubborn with a very pronounced sense of right and wrong; a sincere concern for morality, honesty, and caring; and a profound sense of justice.

I believe perfectionism tends to enhance stubbornness in gifted children because many times these children are quite intent on getting the "right answer." This might also be an interfering factor in

social relationships. There is more on this topic in my chapter on perfectionism.

Q. What are some of the common characteristics of gifted children?
A. Please read the list/chart on page 5.

Q. Can you recommend any good books to help me get a better understanding of this whole arena of gifted education? What does it mean?
Whom does it pertain to? Is it elitist?
A. For years, I used James Gallagher's book, *Teaching the Gifted
Child,* 4th ed. (Boston: Allyn and Bacon, 1994), as the main text in
the graduate courses I taught. The book gave a fine overview of the
academic and curricular aspects of educating the gifted. The end of

Common Characteristics of Gifted and Talented

- Able to express self easily, succinctly, and without hesitation. Many times we need to help them "cushion" their responses in respect for other's feelings
- Accomplished across a broad range of skills
- Easy recall of facts and mastery of knowlege presented
- Has a delightful sense of humor, understands and appreciates wit
- Intense concentration and attention in area(s) where interested; can become highly focused and absorbed
- Keen sense of what's right and often sees issues as either black or white
- Likes to assume leadership roles
- Loves learning
- Nonconformist
- Perfectionist
- Persistent (some refer to as stubborn)
- Posesses specific academic aptitudes
- Procrastinator
- Questioning, curious, inquisitive
- Reads several years above grade-level expectations
- Sensitive, intuitive
- Sets high goals and standards for self
- Takes pleasure in inductive learning and synthesis (creativity)
- Verbal (very)

each chapter contained reflective thinking questions, which I particularly liked. However, the text has become quite expensive for many struggling college students, approaching $90 once tax is included.

I also wholeheartedly support two other textbooks in my graduate course: Ellen Winner's *Gifted Children Myths and Realities* (New York: Basic Books, 1996) and Adderholdt and Goldberg's *Perfectionism: What's Bad about Being Too Good?* (Minneapolis: Free Spirit Publishing, 1999).

Q. Do gifted children have the same feelings and thoughts as other children their ages?

A. I believe all children need to be loved, protected, and nourished emotionally and intellectually. Children need to play and laugh. Children need to express themselves and have their thinking and talents supported. Gifted children are no different. Their needs are the same as those of all other children—and more.

Gifted children need to talk through the complexities in their minds. They need to listen to the adults they respect and love, heeding the wisdom and advice of caring parents and teachers. Gifted children need help with time management and organization. They need to be understood.

The Gifted Kids' Survival Guide for Ages 11–18, Galbraith (1983, 17) lists the eight gripes of gifted kids.

The Eight Great Gripes of Gifted Kids

1. The stuff we do in school is too easy and it's boring.
2. Parents (teachers, friends) expect us to be perfect, to "do our best" all the time.
3. Lots of our coursework is irrelevant.
4. Friends who really understand us are few and far between.
5. Peers often tease us about being smart.
6. We feel overwhelmed by the number of things we can do in life.
7. We feel too different, alienated.
8. We worry a lot about world problems and feel helpless to do anything.

Excerpted from *The Gifted Kids' Survival Guide for Ages 11–18*, by Judy Galbraith, © 1983, Free Spirit Publishing, Inc., Minneapolis, Minn., 800-735-7323.

Q. Our ten-year-old daughter Julie was identified in kindergarten by the school district as gifted. She started reading at the age of three and excels in all subject areas. However, she does not seem to set realistic goals for herself and often doesn't complete all her projects. Is this characteristic of gifted children?

A. Yes, indeed, many gifted children want to do, see, and hear everything in sight. Because they have the ability to think and comprehend well beyond their years, these children want to experience it all, and all at once. I used to silently chuckle to myself when many of the students in my self-contained gifted classes would get teacher and parent approval for their long-term research and creativity projects, only to want to switch midstream to pursue other creative ideas!

Parents and teachers can play a huge role in helping gifted children set realistic goals, stay focused, and manage their time wisely. These skills become even more crucial as children approach middle and high school years.

I deal with time management and study skills quite extensively in chapter 4. You'll find some good tips there, so keep reading.

Q. What exactly does an IQ have to do with a person being gifted? Our son measured a 128 IQ in the school testing and was denied access to the gifted program in fourth grade. Apparently, because he didn't measure an IQ of 130+, he couldn't be classified as gifted. He always earns straight As or A+s on all his tests and report cards and is considered a leader amongst his classmates. I'm stumped as to why Clint would be denied entrance into the gifted program!

A. I've heard this same unfortunate story for many years throughout my career. The traditional gifted programs were set up for students who met the following three criteria:

- IQ of 130+
- Stanine of 8 or 9 on Standardized Achievement Test scores
- Teacher recommendation

This was the problem with exclusive programs in the past. You were either in or out, gifted or not! Although IQ (Intelligence Quotient) is a standardized measure of your potential to do well in the academic arena, it does not measure the full range of abilities, including creativity. IQ primarily measures your ability with language and numbers.

This is why an inclusive process for educating the gifted is so much better and healthier than an exclusive program in our educational system. Through the use of curriculum compacting, differentiation, and acceleration, we can service all kids, including the gifted!

Q. Our three gifted teenagers have absolutely no common sense whatsoever. I'm beginning to believe in the phrase, "If their heads weren't attached to their bodies, they'd walk off without them!" How can this be true if they're gifted?

A. If your children were right here with me now, I'd say to them, "Welcome to the club!" Giftedness has to do with the ability of children to perform or show the potential for performing at remarkably high levels of accomplishment when compared with others of their age, experience, or environment (Ross 1993, 26).

Giftedness has nothing to do with common sense. Common sense is more than likely linked to your children's learning styles. I'm guessing their style would be abstract random.

For years when I was growing up, my father would exasperatingly say to me "How can someone who is so smart lose so many things and not have common sense?" Being proactive, Dad put up a key ring by the door and double-checked me when I arrived home to be sure I would place my keys there—otherwise, I would place my keys anywhere in the house without thinking, then search frantically for them later when I needed them.

Simple but practical solutions such as this really do help children whose thinking styles are abstract random. The upside to this style is often an easy ability to think "out of the box" and be creative.

Anytime you help your children with organization, time management, and just slowing them down to talk through "common sense" issues, you'll be giving them a great gift and service.

I know, I've been there, done that, and was forever grateful for the help . . . and still am!

2

PROGRAMMING AND CURRICULUM DEVELOPMENT IN GIFTED EDUCATION

A variety of program models and curriculum developments have developed over the past two decades to help in the appropriate education of our high-achieving, cognitively gifted students. Ideally, your school district is providing training and assistance to your teachers so that all students may benefit from these advances.

PROGRAM MODELS FOR EDUCATING THE GIFTED

Enrichment in Regular Classroom

Enrichment refers to the classroom teacher providing additional work and/or activities/materials for individual students who already have mastered the grade-level materials.

Curriculum Differentiation

Curriculum differentiation is a teaching approach that focuses on the higher-level thinking skills of application, synthesis, and evaluation and can be applied in the educational areas of content, process, and product in the learning environment. Teachers respond to where students' mastery levels are, not at grade-level expectations.

Curriculum Compacting

Students may pretest out of units of study they already have mastered at an earlier time in their educational development than their peers. This gives the children time to pursue other studies of interests or more advanced materials in the curriculum being currently studied. This gives time and freedom to students whose achievement is above grade-level expectations.

Independent Study

Independent study is guided and directed by the teacher, and can provide a wonderful opportunity for a student to develop an interest or talent that might not be provided in the regular curriculum. This *does not* mean sending gifted students off on their own, unsupervised, without instruction, guidance, and help.

Resource Room

This model reminds me of the classic quote, "Help! I'm gifted more than one hour a week!" This is the criticism most often levied against the resource room model, where gifted students are pulled out of their regular classrooms a specified amount of time per day or week. A teaching expert provides direct instruction for the gifted students. Many times, students are required to make up the work they missed in the regular classroom while they were gone. Thus, the resource room model can become a punishment for being gifted.

Consultant Teacher

This model provides the classroom teacher and gifted students with an education expert right in the classroom, servicing a direct support for instruction. Curriculum differentiation is the primary goal of the teacher and consultant for all the students.

Special Schools

These provide a secondary education for high ability, high-achieving students.

Mentors

A mentor is a wonderful "gift" for any child. A student may access a mentor by leaving the school on a specific day or days for a specified amount of time. The mentor is a specialist in the area of expertise or focused interest of the child. I dearly wish I had a mentor growing up. What a gift that would have been!

Acceleration

This refers to moving the student to a level of study that matches his or her aptitude and mastery levels in one or more curricular areas. This can be highly effective, especially by use of compacting at the elementary level.

Advanced Placement Courses

AP courses were originally designed to provide gifted students with the opportunity to receive college-level course credit while still in high school. Educational Testing Service provides an opportunity for students to take a test in a specified subject area and students will usually receive college credit if they score either a 4 or 5.

WHO MURDERED THE MINDS OF GIFTED CHILDREN?

PROFESSOR DULL, IN THE CLASSROOM, WITH REPETITIVE DRILLS

Q. The school district my three children are in is constantly fighting over how to best service gifted children. Many of the parents want their children identified, pulled out, and serviced in a self-contained classroom. Teachers want the students to remain in their own classrooms. What is the best way to educate gifted children? I don't want my children losing out.

A. Good news. It doesn't matter how your gifted children are serviced for their best education. It does matter that they are! A three-year study in Framingham, Massachusetts, looked at educating gifted children using three program models. In 1984, the National Diffusion Network published the results from this study that compared the effectiveness of these three major program models used in delivering Project SAGE instruction to academically gifted students: separate classrooms (self-contained), resource room, and the consultant teacher model (Cymerman and Modest 1984).

The research found that students who participated in the pilot program, using any of the three program models, performed at a significantly higher level in higher-order thinking skills and academics than their peers in the control group who did not receive special services.

Schools can use a variety of program models to provide appropriate instruction for gifted students. The key is providing the instruction!

Q. All four of our children went through a self-contained gifted program in a suburban district of Rochester, New York. While my husband and I were very happy with the teachers and education our children received, the students certainly were very isolated from the remainder of the school population and it was obvious there was open disdain (jealousy) toward the gifted class from the other students and teachers. How do you feel about self-contained gifted classes and their effect on the social interaction and development of self and peer relationships?

A. Your situation is of particular interest to me because I started my teaching career with gifted education in a fourth-grade, self-contained classroom. The students selected for the program were bussed from all over the district to my classroom.

As an educator, I believed this program model was an excellent way to service the academic and emotional needs of gifted children, and in many ways, it was. However, the resentment of other teachers toward a classroom of gifted students was enormous. The disdain was not just covert, it was blatantly overt! The unfriendliness from parents of children who were not selected for this district's gifted program was just as bad or worse!

Few teachers who chose to teach in the district's gifted program lasted more than one, two, or three years because of the prejudice and isolation.

I survived eighteen years. I believed that all children deserved to become all they are capable of becoming, including very bright children, and I was willing to suffer the indignities of others to support my beliefs and the educational rights of these children.

The self-contained gifted program became such a "hot bed" of political uproar, the district finally did away with it in the 1990s.

I continued to educationally serve the gifted students in my heterogeneously grouped classrooms both at the elementary and middle school levels.

I clearly remember the resource room teacher saying to me, "Now that you'll be having a heterogeneously grouped classroom, you'll find that you'll be spending an inordinate amount of time with the slower achieving students."

My mental response was, "Over my dead body!" You see, I believed in giving equal amounts of time to my students. I would certainly "help" the slower achieving students, but I would also "help" the higher achieving students whom I was trying to educate at the appropriate aptitude levels. To do less was unacceptable in my mind.

As time progressed, I came to support an inclusive process for the education of gifted students, rather than an exclusive program. This process was a healthier approach community-wide. Rather than being in or out, gifted or not gifted, the inclusive process did not exclude children and families; rather, it included and encompassed the districtwide community.

A large number of my former "self-contained" gifted students and their parents have kept in touch with me. We're all pretty much in agreement that while a self-contained program academically serves gifted children, emotionally it seems to encourage negative issues with staff, other students, and administrators, for the teacher of self-contained gifted as well as the students.

SERVING THE GIFTED: AN INCLUSIVE PROCESS RATHER THAN AN EXCLUSIVE PROGRAM!

Q. Can you explain to me what curriculum compacting is?
A. Sure. So many of our gifted children daily suffer the indignities of doing curricular work and endless hours of homework on material they already know. In fact, research on curriculum compacting shows that teachers could eliminate as much as 40 to 50 percent of the usual material without affecting achievement scores in reading, math, computation, social studies, and spelling (Reis 1994). Basically, curriculum compacting excuses high-ability students from plowing through material they have already mastered.

Not surprising to many educators or parents of gifted children, the National Commission on Excellence in Education released a searing report in 1983 on the condition of American educational institutions,

gifted student

finding that 50 percent of all gifted students did not perform to their tested potential.

What is curriculum compacting exactly? It is a wonderful strategy used by gifted education specialists to service not only high-achieving students, but all students whose abilities or achievements surpass those of their grade-level peers. By using compacting, students' achievements are assessed by pretesting their curriculum knowledge before a unit of study. Why make children study materials they already know and have mastered? To me, this is pure common sense! The educator can then set up a plan of study to include materials the student may not already know and develop units of study to challenge and develop the child's cognitive base. This is where a blend of enrichment and acceleration complement educational excellence for our country's children.

Q. Does differentiation serve the needs of the gifted? Our district's entire focus in their gifted program is differentiation. Is that all there is?
A. Differentiation is a part of the process needed to service the educational needs of gifted children, not the complete process. In my latest article, "The Missing Ingredient for Servicing Gifted Children," I talk directly about this problem. Just as districts in the '70s, '80s, and '90s went overboard with enrichment as the answer for educating gifted children, school districts are now going overboard with differentiation as the sole answer for educating gifted children. Another key part of the process is servicing gifted children at their aptitude levels, which could entail acceleration, compacting, enrichment, or possible grade skipping.

When you have a second grader whose reading comprehension and vocabulary levels are at the eighth-grade level, exposing him to more and more books at the second-grade reading level is not going to expand his cognitive learning, nor is it going to expand his vocabulary and comprehension.

> # Acceleration & Enrichment = Meeting gifted students' instructional needs

Until we can help teachers and administrators feel more comfortable with compacting and acceleration at the elementary and middle school levels, I do not believe we are fully servicing our gifted children. At the high school level, AP (Advanced Placement) courses are readily acceptable.

Differentiation is a start. Credit goes to your school district for supporting it. Encourage them to expand their process for servicing their gifted.

Q. How do you know if you are challenging your gifted students?

A. This is a genuine and common concern of many teachers who are currently being overburdened with inclusion classrooms whose numbers exceed thirty children, with academic and aptitude ranges varying from three to five years below grade level up to eight to ten years beyond grade level. Ideally, districts are providing aides as well as gifted and talented facilitators to help these teachers with curriculum compacting and differentiation as a start.

You know you are not challenging your gifted students, if you are

1. having them help the slower-achieving students in the classroom on a regular or daily basis,
2. having them do grade-level work and they almost always finish first or before most of their classmates,
3. if you give them "enrichment" activities that are always at grade-level expectations,
4. if they are getting straight As in achievement because they already know the material being taught,
5. if their writing and speaking reflect "rote memorization," and
6. if the work they are producing is at the lower level of thinking on Bloom's Taxonomy: knowledge, comprehension, and application.

You are challenging your gifted students, if you are

1. pretesting their knowledge base and compacting their curriculum so that they are learning at their aptitude and achievement levels,
2. if you are considering the alternatives of enrichment combined with acceleration and grade-level curriculum,
3. if they are spending somewhat equal amounts of time in class learning and completing appropriate assignments as their peers achieving at grade level,

4. if their writing and speaking reflect a higher-level thinking order, and
5. if the work they are producing is at the higher level of Bloom's Taxonomy: analysis, synthesis, and evaluation.

I've known some districts that differentiate their curriculum for the benefit of their gifted students and expect only these children to produce at the application, synthesis, and evaluation levels, while the other students are not expected to achieve at these levels at all! Here we should revise our thinking, as I truly believe we should be training and expecting all of our students to produce at these higher levels of thinking!

Q. My son always finishes his work ahead of the rest of his class, so the teacher uses him as a helper/tutor for the other children. Although I encourage Greg to be kind and helpful, shouldn't he be working on his own projects and interests while he's waiting for his classmates to finish their assignments?

A. Yes! Helping others is certainly a valuable, caring, and necessary activity for all of us throughout our lives. In school, such behavior should be encouraged and respected. However, if done to the exclusion of self-achievement, learning and being taught at the appropriate ability level is not right. If we rob Peter to pay Paul, where is the justice for Peter? If Greg is "tutoring/helping" his classmates daily, where is his educational justice in the development of his abilities?

Compacting and small group instruction should begin for Greg and other high-achieving children as early as kindergarten. It's their educational right.

Q. My child comes home every day from kindergarten and asks me why she can't learn something new in school. She used to be a very happy and bubbly little girl. Now she's losing her enthusiasm for school. Eugenia was reading by the time she was three years old. In school, she must sit through daily lessons on the letters of the alphabet. When I've talked to her teacher about this, she says kindergarten is a time to learn socialization skills and there are far too many students for her (the teacher) to do individual lessons with my child. Can't something be done to help with the education of the five-year-olds who already get along with their peers and know the curriculum two or three years before entering school? This just doesn't seem fair or right. Do you agree?

A. I not only agree with you, I truly empathize with you and feel your frustration as a parent and a teacher. I am saddened by the number of schools that do not provide an education for students at their appropriate aptitude and achievement levels. We've come way too far with Bloom's Taxonomy, differentiation models, gifted program models, compacting, acceleration, independent study, learning centers, etc., to have children repeating skills and academics in school they've learned months or years before.

Although I do empathize with the increasing load and expectations placed on teachers in our classrooms from year to year, staff development courses are available and consultants can readily be hired to come into districts and actually help the educators with initial compacting and differentiation.

Many districts are now hiring gifted and talented coordinators to help with district curriculum development, teaching training, and student support. Beware of a district coordinator who doesn't want to work with the children at all. This may indicate a "hands-off" rather than "hands-on" philosophy.

Q. It seems that our school district focuses on "enrichment" activities to fulfill its obligations to our gifted children. In mathematics, my son has scored eight years beyond his grade-level peers. Doesn't it make sense he should be doing math work at a more difficult and more complex level other than enrichment exercises at his fourth-grade level?!?

A. Absolutely! In a positive sense, enrichment activities are meant to extend the curriculum and regular school-day programs, providing more in-depth experiences, uses of creativity, and thought-provoking exercises. In theory, enrichment would benefit any child. In practice, many school districts have gone overboard with the use of "enrichment" as the sole means of servicing its gifted population. I have seen many gifted elementary students over the years "enriched" with grade-level activities until the children wanted to regurgitate. Finishing their work ahead of their peers became a source of "punishment" for gifted kids. They would be expected to move onto one of the "enrichment centers" and do "more work," or be expected to help the slower-achieving students, thus diminishing the positive effects of completing the required assignment or project.

This use of enrichment is often controlled by the teacher and seldom gives the high-achieving student time to pursue her own interests and talents.

We need to look at a balance. There are hundreds of thousands of exceptional learning or enrichment centers throughout the classrooms in our country's schools. They should be a "part of" the students' day or a viable option, not something required once the day's activities are completed.

If we are educating our gifted students at their appropriate aptitude levels, via compacting or acceleration, for example, then it would be highly unlikely that these children would be finishing their daily assignments so far ahead of their peers. And if they do, why not let them choose how they would like to spend the additional time while their peers are completing their assignments? If someone loves to read, let him read. If Mark loves writing computer programs, why not let him work on the computer? If Olivia is a gifted artist, let her work on her illustration on the easel in the art room the art teacher has provided for her. And if John is simply tired, putting his head down on his desk for fifteen minutes and napping could refresh him physically and mentally for the remainder of the day!

Q. Although I credit our school district with trying to service gifted children, the process seems to be failing at the elementary and middle school levels. Even the AP courses at the high school seem to pile on more and more work, without giving equivalent grade point averages. Our daughter is a very gifted writer and is becoming frustrated with the additional writing assignments she is given because of her talent. At this point, I'm willing to home school, but I'm afraid Meghan will miss out on social and peer relationships. Please advise.

A. I certainly can support your decision to home school after having a very brilliant graduate student in one of my graduate classes who was home schooling her own two very gifted children. Until that time, I must confess, I was a product of many of the same stereotypes that educators and the general public have about home schooling.

Every semester, I now invite three home-schooling parents in for a presentation to my graduate students in "Teaching the Gifted K–12." My students always rave about the session for weeks that follow.

Mary Fran runs a very structured learning day for her elementary-aged children, with subject instruction scheduled at certain times and a mini-classroom set up in her basement.

Rikki's children's days are unstructured. Her middle and high school children (as well as she) sleep into a natural waking each morning. The children and the mother have a quiet part of the house to study, create, read, etc. Mutually agreed-upon times are issued when help with instruction will be given. Trips to the local library or museums can be all day, to benefit each family member.

Jennifer has been home schooling for religious and family reasons. Her two high school children are now attending the public school and are academic and social leaders in their classes. Jennifer's sixth grader is being home schooled and "aces" the state and district tests she takes at home each year.

Academic and social events are scheduled regularly for home schoolers throughout the county. The myth that home schoolers would miss the socialization acquired in public schools just isn't true. I was awed by the number of events and volunteer time donated for the benefit of all home-schooled children by these parents.

I respect home schooling as a positive and family-oriented alternative for the education of your children. I encourage you to try it if that's where your heart is leaning.

Q. The staff development monies in our district are being used almost exclusively for the training of teachers in 4-MAT. Everyone is expected to speak and write using the 4-MAT lingo, to the exclusion of all else. Is this training model the best way to educate gifted children?

A. No. 4-MAT is one of many excellent program models being used to enhance educators' understanding and development of children's and adults' learning styles as well as teaching strategies. I would be a bit leery of any district that promotes one style of teacher training to the exclusion of all others. It's a little bit like expecting all children to think and produce the same way, the opposite of what education should be doing—enhancing the thinking, production, and creativity of the individual at her best levels.

I encourage you to encourage your children's school district to be more flexible in its teaching training regimen. There are many excellent methods and techniques available to use in the educating of our children. Some methods work for some, others work equally as well or better for others. Good luck!

Q. My child has been tested to be reading at the sixth-grade comprehension level, yet she is forced to read the same curricular materials as the other student peers in the second-grade classroom. How can I get instructional help for her to ensure she's extending her knowledge and ability base?

A. Don't despair. I have very successfully used a variety of supplemental reading programs throughout my career to enhance gifted and independent readers. One of them is Accelerated Reader. Accelerated Reader is a sensory information system that manages literature-based reading practice. With more than thirty thousand titles for children to select from, this easily accessible software program supports the actual reading level of participating students. Children in first grade whose cognitive reading level far surpasses their peers by two, three, four, or even five years needn't by slowed down by "grade-level" reading lessons and expectations. The same is true for all the other elementary, middle, and high school-level children.

Although Accelerated Reader was first designed as a software literature program for gifted children, it has now expanded to support test scores for all levels.

Q. Do you have any favorite books you could recommend for my eleven-year-old son to read? He is always so busy completing daily homework assignments, he doesn't have time for pleasure reading. The little time he does have, the books need to be good! He used to love pleasure reading. Help!

A. Yes! I absolutely love and adore the Newbery books and I think parents would enjoy reading these yearly award-winning books right along with their children. The reading levels range approximately between 4.5 and 6.0 and I've used some of the titles with gifted second- and third-grade readers as well as middle school children.

NEWBERY AWARD-WINNING BOOKS (1922–2002)

The Newbery Award for original and creative work in the field of children's books was first awarded in 1922 to Hendrik Willem van Loon for *The Story of Mankind*. Since its inception, seventy-nine award-winning books and well over two hundred honor books have received the prestigious John Newbery Medal.

My personal all-time Newbery favorite is Robert C. O'Brien's *Mrs. Frisby and the Rats of NIMH*, followed by Spinelli's *Maniac Magee*, Paterson's *Bridge to Terabithia*, and Raskin's *The Westing Game*. I've read all the Newberys.

I still remember sitting up in bed exclaiming, "No, please, no!" when Leslie accidentally died in Terebithia. Every year, I read "Mrs. Frisby" to my classes, whether teaching middle school level, intermediate, or primary children, and the students loved it.

The Newbery books present dilemmas, problem solving, life experiences, family support, and interactions with enriched vocabulary, ad infinatum. I've yet to meet a gifted student who wasn't intrigued and delighted with the Newbery books.

While I was teaching a self-contained fourth-grade class of gifted students (many years ago), I developed a Newbery Club to accelerate reading of fine literature in my classroom. I applied to our school's PTA for a $300 grant to get started and received it. With parent volunteers, we began by modeling a Newbery membership card after our school's computer club membership card. We made twenty-five buttons with our school's button machine, using a picture of the Newbery bronze medal designed by René Paul Chambellan back in 1921.

Great news! Within two years, the Newbery Club became a school-wide incentive reading program for our fourth, fifth, and sixth grades, sponsored by the profits from the library's yearly book fair. We also had third graders reading Newberys, as well as five gifted second graders. In fact, one of the third graders broke all the school records initially established and received all the prizes we had to offer by the end of fourth grade. We reworked the award system and extended the top award to the reading of 150 Newbery books and prizes that could be accumulated throughout the child's schooling! The Newbery Club became a wonderful, schoolwide, outstanding reading incentive!

I have included a copy of our original Newbery Club Award Sheet and a listing of the award-winning books, 1922–2000, for you.

Happy reading and awarding!

---

* * * AWARDS * * *

Newbery Club Book Awards

READ! READ! READ!

READ/CONFERENCE		PRIZES	
I.	3 Books	I.	A Membership Card and Newbery Button
II.	6 Books	II.	1 Free Newbery Book of Your Choice
III.	10 Books	III.	1 More Fabulous, Exciting, Adventurous Newbery Book!!!
IV.	15 Books	IV.	1 Cool Newbery T-Shirt!
V.	25 Books	V.	2 More Newbery Books!
VI.	35 Books	VI.	Another 2 Books!!
VII.	50 Books	VII.	3 Free Books and an Ice Cream Sundae of your Choice
VIII.	65 Books	VIII.	2 Free Newberys
XI.	80 Books	XI.	A Trophy
X.	90 Books	X.	3 Free Books
XI.	100 Books	XI.	1 Free Book for the Remainder of the School Year!

CONGRATULATIONS !

Newbery Medal Winners, 1922–2002:

- 2002: *Single Shard* by Linda Park (Houghton Mifflin)
- 2001: *Year Down Yonder* by Richard Peck (Dial)
- 2000: *Bud, Not Buddy* by Christopher Paul Curtis (Delacorte)
- 1999: *Holes* by Louis Sachar (Frances Foster)
- 1998: *Out of the Dust* by Karen Hesse (Scholastic)
- 1997: *The View from Saturday* by E. L. Konigsburg (Jean Karl/Atheneum)
- 1996: *The Midwife's Apprentice* by Karen Cushman (Clarion)
- 1995: *Walk Two Moons* by Sharon Creech (HarperCollins)
- 1994: *The Giver* by Lois Lowry (Houghton)
- 1993: *Missing May* by Cynthia Rylant (Jackson/Orchard)
- 1992: *Shiloh* by Phyllis Reynolds Naylor (Atheneum)
- 1991: *Maniac Magee* by Jerry Spinelli (Little, Brown)
- 1990: *Number the Stars* by Lois Lowry (Houghton)
- 1989: *Joyful Noise: Poems for Two Voices* by Paul Fleischman (Harper)
- 1988: *Lincoln: A Photobiography* by Russell Freedman (Clarion)
- 1987: *The Whipping Boy* by Sid Fleischman (Greenwillow)
- 1986: *Sarah, Plain and Tall* by Patricia MacLachlan (Harper)
- 1985: *The Hero and the Crown* by Robin McKinley (Greenwillow)
- 1984: *Dear Mr. Henshaw* by Beverly Cleary (Morrow)
- 1983: *Dicey's Song* by Cynthia Voigt (Atheneum)
- 1982: *A Visit to William Blake's Inn: Poems for Innocent and Experienced Travelers* by Nancy Willard (Harcourt)
- 1981: *Jacob Have I Loved* by Katherine Paterson (Crowell)
- 1980: *A Gathering of Days: A New England Girl's Journal, 1830–1832* by Joan W. Blos (Scribner)
- 1979: *The Westing Game* by Ellen Raskin (Dutton)
- 1978: *Bridge to Terabithia* by Katherine Paterson (Crowell)
- 1977: *Roll of Thunder, Hear My Cry* by Mildred D. Taylor (Dial)
- 1976: *The Grey King* by Susan Cooper (McElderry/Atheneum)
- 1975: *M. C. Higgins, the Great* by Virginia Hamilton (Macmillan)
- 1974: *The Slave Dancer* by Paula Fox (Bradbury)
- 1973: *Julie of the Wolves* by Jean Craighead George (Harper)
- 1972: *Mrs. Frisby and the Rats of NIMH* by Robert C. O'Brien (Atheneum)
- 1971: *Summer of the Swans* by Betsy Byars (Viking)
- 1970: *Sounder* by William H. Armstrong (Harper)
- 1969: *The High King* by Lloyd Alexander (Holt)
- 1968: *From the Mixed-Up Files of Mrs. Basil E. Frankweiler* by E. L. Konigsburg (Atheneum)
- 1967: *Up a Road Slowly* by Irene Hunt (Follett)
- 1966: *I, Juan de Pareja* by Elizabeth Borton de Trevino (Farrar)
- 1965: *Shadow of a Bull* by Maia Wojciechowska (Atheneum)
- 1964: *It's Like This, Cat* by Emily Neville (Harper)
- 1963: *A Wrinkle in Time* by Madeleine L'Engle (Farrar)
- 1962: *The Bronze Bow* by Elizabeth George Speare (Houghton)
- 1961: *Island of the Blue Dolphins* by Scott O'Dell (Houghton)
- 1960: *Onion John* by Joseph Krumgold (Crowell)
- 1959: *The Witch of Blackbird Pond* by Elizabeth George Speare (Houghton)
- 1958: *Rifles for Watie* by Harold Keith (Crowell)

- 1957: *Miracles on Maple Hill* by Virginia Sorenson (Harcourt)
- 1956: *Carry On, Mr. Bowditch* by Jean Lee Latham (Houghton)
- 1955: *The Wheel on the School* by Meindert DeJong (Harper)
- 1954: *...And Now Miguel* by Joseph Krumgold (Crowell)
- 1953: *Secret of the Andes* by Ann Nolan Clark (Viking)
- 1952: *Ginger Pye* by Eleanor Estes (Harcourt)
- 1951: *Amos Fortune, Free Man* by Elizabeth Yates (Dutton)
- 1950: *The Door in the Wall* by Marguerite de Angeli (Doubleday)
- 1949: *King of the Wind* by Marguerite Henry (Rand McNally)
- 1948: *The Twenty-One Balloons* by William Pène du Bois (Viking)
- 1947: *Miss Hickory* by Carolyn Sherwin Bailey (Viking)
- 1946: *Strawberry Girl* by Lois Lenski (Lippincott)
- 1945: *Rabbit Hill* by Robert Lawson (Viking)
- 1944: *Johnny Tremain* by Esther Forbes (Houghton)
- 1943: *Adam of the Road* by Elizabeth Janet Gray (Viking)
- 1942: *The Matchlock Gun* by Walter Edmonds (Dodd)
- 1941: *Call It Courage* by Armstrong Sperry (Macmillan)
- 1940: *Daniel Boone* by James Daugherty (Viking)
- 1939: *Thimble Summer* by Elizabeth Enright (Rinehart)
- 1938: *The White Stag* by Kate Seredy (Viking)
- 1937: *Roller Skates* by Ruth Sawyer (Viking)
- 1936: *Caddie Woodlawn* by Carol Ryrie Brink (Macmillan)
- 1935: *Dobry* by Monica Shannon (Viking)
- 1934: *Invincible Louisa: The Story of the Author of Little Women* by Cornelia Meigs (Little, Brown)
- 1933: *Young Fu of the Upper Yangtze* by Elizabeth Lewis (Winston)
- 1932: *Waterless Mountain* by Laura Adams Armer (Longmans)
- 1931: *The Cat Who Went to Heaven* by Elizabeth Coatsworth (Macmillan)
- 1930: *Hitty, Her First Hundred Years* by Rachel Field (Macmillan)
- 1929: *The Trumpeter of Krakow* by Eric P. Kelly (Macmillan)
- 1928: *Gay Neck, the Story of a Pigeon* by Dhan Gopal Mukerji (Dutton)
- 1927: *Smoky, the Cowhorse* by Will James (Scribner)
- 1926: *Shen of the Sea* by Arthur Bowie Chrisman (Dutton)
- 1925: *Tales from Silver Lands* by Charles Finger (Doubleday)
- 1924: *The Dark Frigate* by Charles Hawes (Little, Brown)
- 1923: *The Voyages of Doctor Dolittle* by Hugh Lofting (Lippincott)
- 1922: *The Story of Mankind* by Hendrik Willem van Loon (Liveright)

For further information on the Newbery Medal Winners, check this Internet address at www.ala.org/alsc/nquick.html.

CALDECOTT MEDAL WINNERS (1938–2002)

In conjunction with the John Newbery Awards for prestigious children's literature, the first Caldecott Medal was awarded to illustrator Dorothy P. Lathrop for *Animals of the Bible*, a picture book in 1938. This award is presented yearly to the artist creating the most distinguished American picture book for children published in the United States. The medal is given in honor of Randolph Caldecott, a nineteenth-century English illustrator.

I have used many of the Caldecott books for my creative writing lessons over the years, at all grade levels, my favorite being Van Allsburg's *The Polar Express*, 1986.

I have also used these beautifully illustrated books with my students whose gifts are in the artistic arena of giftedness.

While I toyed with starting a Caldecott Club similar to our Newbery Club to award our school's gifted artists, I didn't . . . one of my regrets. However, I hope this chapter spurs one or more of you creative parents or art educators reading this book to develop your own Caldecott Clubs for your school. Please let me know if you do. My heart will be happy!

ALSC (Association for Library Service to Children): Caldecott Medal Winners 1938–2002

- 2002: *The Three Pigs* by David Wiesner (Clarion)
- 2001: *So You Want to be President* by Judith St. George (Philomel)
- 2000: *Joseph Had a Little Overcoat* by Simms Taback (Viking)
- 1999: *Snowflake Bentley*, illustrated by Mary Azarian; text by Jacqueline Briggs Martin (Houghton)
- 1998: *Rapunzel* by Paul O. Zelinsky (Dutton)
- 1997: *Golem* by David Wisniewski (Clarion)
- 1996: *Officer Buckle and Gloria* by Peggy Rathmann (Putnam)
- 1995: *Smoky Night*, illustrated by David Diaz; text: Eve Bunting (Harcourt)
- 1994: *Grandfather's Journey*, text and illustrations by Allen Say, edited by Walter Lorraine (Houghton)
- 1993: *Mirette on the High Wire* by Emily Arnold McCully (Putnam)
- 1992: *Tuesday* by David Wiesner (Clarion)
- 1991: *Black and White* by David Macaulay (Houghton)
- 1990: *Lon Po Po: A Red-Riding Hood Story from China* by Ed Young (Philomel)
- 1989: *Song and Dance Man*, illustrated by Stephen Gammell; text by Karen Ackerman (Knopf)
- 1988: *Owl Moon*, illustrated by John Schoenherr; text by Jane Yolen (Philomel)
- 1987: *Hey, Al*, illustrated by Richard Egielski; text by Arthur Yorinks (Farrar)
- 1986: *The Polar Express* by Chris Van Allsburg (Houghton)
- 1985: *Saint George and the Dragon*, illustrated by Trina Schart Hyman; text retold by Margaret Hodges (Little, Brown)
- 1984: *The Glorious Flight: Across the Channel with Louis Bleriot* by Alice and Martin Provensen (Viking)
- 1983: *Shadow*, translated and illustrated by Marcia Brown; original text in French by Blaise Cendrars (Scribner)
- 1982: *Jumanji* by Chris Van Allsburg (Houghton)
- 1981: *Fables* by Arnold Lobel (Harper)
- 1980: *Ox-Cart Man*, illustrated by Barbara Cooney; text by Donald Hall (Viking)

- 1979: *The Girl Who Loved Wild Horses* by Paul Goble (Bradbury)
- 1978: *Noah's Ark* by Peter Spier (Doubleday)
- 1977: *Ashanti to Zulu: African Traditions*, illustrated by Leo and Diane Dillon; text by Margaret Musgrove (Dial)
- 1976: *Why Mosquitoes Buzz in People's Ears*, illustrated by Leo and Diane Dillon; text retold by Verna Aardema (Dial)
- 1975: *Arrow to the Sun* by Gerald McDermott (Viking)
- 1974: *Duffy and the Devil*, illustrated by Margot Zemach; retold by Harve Zemach (Farrar)
- 1973: *The Funny Little Woman*, illustrated by Blair Lent; text retold by Arlene Mosel (Dutton)
- 1972: *One Fine Day*, retold and illustrated by Nonny Hogrogian (Macmillan)
- 1971: *A Story A Story*, retold and illustrated by Gail E. Haley (Atheneum)
- 1970: *Sylvester and the Magic Pebble* by William Steig (Windmill Books)
- 1969: *The Fool of the World and the Flying Ship*, illustrated by Uri Shulevitz; text retold by Arthur Ransome (Farrar)
- 1968: *Drummer Hoff*, illustrated by Ed Emberley; text adapted by Barbara Emberley (Prentice-Hall)
- 1967: *Sam, Bangs & Moonshine* by Evaline Ness (Holt)
- 1966: *Always Room for One More*, illustrated by Nonny Hogrogian; text by Sorche Nic Leodhas, pseud. [Leclair Alger] (Holt)
- 1965: *May I Bring a Friend?* illustrated by Beni Montresor; text by Beatrice Schenk de Regniers (Atheneum)
- 1964: *Where the Wild Things Are* by Maurice Sendak (Harper)
- 1963: *The Snowy Day* by Ezra Jack Keats (Viking)
- 1962: *Once a Mouse*, retold and illustrated by Marcia Brown (Scribner)
- 1961: *Baboushka and the Three Kings*, illustrated by Nicolas Sidjakov; text: Ruth Robbins (Parnassus)
- 1960: *Nine Days to Christmas*, illustrated by Marie Hall Ets by text: Marie Hall Ets and Aurora Labastida (Viking)
- 1959: *Chanticleer and the Fox*, illustrated by Barbara Cooney; text adapted from Chaucer's Canterbury Tales by Barbara Cooney (Crowell)
- 1958: *Time of Wonder* by Robert McCloskey (Viking)
- 1957: *A Tree Is Nice*, illustrated by Marc Simont; text: Janice Udry (Harper)
- 1956: *Frog Went A-Courtin'*, illustrated by Feodor Rojankovsky; text retold by John Langstaff (Harcourt)
- 1955: *Cinderella, or the Little Glass Slipper*, illustrated by Marcia Brown; text translated from Charles Perrault by Marcia Brown (Scribner)
- 1954: *Madeline's Rescue* by Ludwig Bemelmans (Viking)
- 1953: *The Biggest Bear* by Lynd Ward (Houghton)
- 1952: *Finders Keepers*, illustrated by Nicolas, pseud. [Nicholas Mordvinoff]; text by Will, pseud. [William Lipkind] (Harcourt)
- 1951: *The Egg Tree* by Katherine Milhous (Scribner)
- 1950: *Song of the Swallows* by Leo Politi (Scribner)
- 1949: *The Big Snow* by Berta and Elmer Hader (Macmillan)
- 1948: *White Snow, Bright Snow*, illustrated by Roger Duvoisin; text by Alvin Tresselt (Lothrop)
- 1947: *The Little Island*, illustrated by Leonard Weisgard; text by Golden MacDonald, pseud. [Margaret Wise Brown] (Doubleday)
- 1946: *The Rooster Crows* by Maude and Miska Petersham (Macmillan)

(continued)

ALSC: Caldecott Medal Winners 1938–2002 *(continued)*

- 1945: *Prayer for a Child*, illustrated by Elizabeth Orton Jones; text by Rachel Field (Macmillan)
- 1944: *Many Moons*, illustrated by Louis Slobodkin; text by James Thurber (Harcourt)
- 1943: *The Little House* by Virginia Lee Burton (Houghton)
- 1942: *Make Way for Ducklings* by Robert McCloskey (Viking)
- 1941: *They Were Strong and Good*, by Robert Lawson (Viking)
- 1940: *Abraham Lincoln* by Ingri and Edgar Parin d'Aulaire (Doubleday)
- 1939: *Mei Li* by Thomas Handforth (Doubleday)
- 1938: *Animals of the Bible, A Picture Book*, illustrated by Dorothy P. Lathrop; text selected by Helen Dean Fish (Lippincott)

You may also access more information about the Caldecotts and Newberys on the Internet at www.ala.org/alsc/cquidc.html.

Q. I have three very precocious and gifted children, ages seven, ten, and twelve. All were reading fluently before entering public schools and continue to have a love for reading. Can you suggest any books where the primary characters are gifted? I'd like to encourage my children through gifted heroes/heroines as role models in literature.

A. Yes! I certainly have my favorite: the *Anne of Green Gables* series. Not only was Anne spunky, bright, gifted, and mischievous (in a good sort of way, of course), she was also a redhead, like myself. I was in my glory reading L. M. Montgomery's books. Just two years ago, I started asking my graduate students in "Teaching the Gifted K–12" who their favorite gifted characters in a book were. Table 2.3 lists of the more popular book titles they suggested, whose protagonists were gifted in one or more areas.

> "Art opens up
>
> the magic of the mind."
>
> -Gribb

Favorite Books with a Gifted Primary Character

Author	Title	Copyright	Publisher
Bemelmans, Ludwig	Madeline	1976	Viking Penguin
Benzia, Mike	Picasso	1988	Regensteiner
Brighton, Catherine	The Fossil Girl	1999	Millbrook Press
Bush, Timothy	Grant! The Primitive Core Boy	1995	Random House
Cade Bambara, Toni	Raymond's Run	1993	The Creative Company
Carmody, Isabelle	Obernewtyn	1987	Puffin Books
Caswell, Brian	A Cage of Butterflies	1992	University of Queensland Press
Chesworth, Michael	Archibald Frisby	1994	Farrar Straus & Giroux
Cleary, Beverly	Ramona the Brave	1975	Dell
Clements, Andrew	The Landry News	1999	Aladdin Paperbacks
Cohen, Barbara	213 Valentines	1991	Henry Holt
Cooper, Susan	The Dark Is Rising	1973	Collies Books
Dahl, Roald	Charlie and the Chocolate Factory	1964	Alfred Knopf
Dan Myers, Walter	Darnell Rock Reporting	1994	Bantam Doubleday Dell Books for Young Readers
Engel, L.	A Ring of Endless Light	1981	Bantam Doubleday Books
Ericsson Lindgren, Astrid	Pippi Longstocking	1976	Penguin Putnam Books for Young Readers
Estes, Eleanor	The Hundred Dresses	1944/1973	Scholastic
Fleischman, Paul	Weslandia	1999	Candlewick Press
Forbes, Esther	Johnny Tremain	1943	Bantam Doubleday Dell for Young Readers
Galdone, Paul	The Little Red Hen	1991	Houghton Mifflin
Hinton, S. E.	The Outsiders	1997	Viking Penguin
Hodgson Burnett, Frances	A Little Princess	1981	Watermill Press
Hoffmann, Mary	Amazing Grace	1991	Kirkus Associates
Ingalls Wilder, Laura	Little House in the Big Woods	1976	HarperCollins Children's Books
Jacques, Brian	Redwall	1986	Random House
Kallok, Emma	The Diary of Chickabiddy Baby	1999	Scholastic
King-Smith, Dick	A Mouse Called Wolf	1977	Dell Yearling
Klein, Robin	Halfway Across the Galaxy and Turn Left	1985	Puffin Books

(continued)

Favorite Books with a Gifted Primary Character *(continued)*

Author	Title	Copyright	Publisher
Konigsburg, E. L.	The View from Saturday	1996	Aladdin Paperbacks
Lackey, Mercedes	Magic's Pawn	1990	Daw Books
LeGuin, Ursula	The Earthsea Quartet	1993	Puffin Books
Lowry, Lois	Anastasia Krupnik	1981	Bantam Doubleday Dell
Lowry, Lois	The Giver	1993	Bantam Doubleday Dell
McLerran, Alice	Roxaboxen	1991	William Morrow
Montague, Jeanne	Midnight Moon	1985	St. Martin Press
Montgomery, L. M.	Anne of Green Gables	1972	Bantam Books
Moon, Nicole	Lucy's Picture	1995	Dial Books
Noslinger, Christine	Konrad	1976	Andersen Press
Odgers, Sally	Translations in Celadon	1998	HarperCollins
Parish, Peggy	Amelia Bedelia		Scholastic
Potok, Chaim	The Chosen	1976	Fawcett
Rachlin, Ann	Mozart	1992	Barron's Educational Services
Richter, Conrad	The Light in the Forest	1994	Random House
Rowling, J. K.	Harry Potter and the Sorcerer's Stone	1998	Scholastic Trade
Rowling, J. K.	Harry Potter and the Goblet of Fire	2000	Scholastic Press
Salinger, J.D.	The Catcher in the Rye	1991	Little, Brown
Scierzka, Jan	The True Story of the Three Little Pigs	1996	Penguin Putnam Books for Young Readers
Spinelli, Jerry	Maniac Magee	1990	Little Brown
Stewart, Sara	The Gardner	1997	Harper-Collins Canada
Sullivan, Anne, and Helen Keller	Helen Keller	1989	Scholastic
Tusa, Tricia	Bunnies in My Head	1998	University of Texas, M. D. Anderson Cancer Ctr.
White, E. B.	Charlotte's Web	1980	HarperCollins
Williams, Margery	Velveteen Rabbit	1988	Random House
Wise Brown, Margaret	Runaway Bunny	1942	Harper Trophey, Collins
Wynne Jones, Diana	Charmed Life	1989	William Morrow
Wynne Jones, Diana	The Lives of Christopher Chant	1988	Methuen

Q. What do you recommend as excellent literature for gifted teenagers? Both our sons are being "turned off" by the required readings in high school and are quickly losing their lifelong love of reading! **A.** I will never forget my reaction while reading Bach's *Jonathan Livingston Seagull*, when the flock stoned Jonathan to death while he tried to share the incredible feat of breaking the sound barrier! In retrospect, what a good lesson to learn about society's often rejection of brilliance, achievement, and change!

I began asking my graduate students what their favorite book as a teenager was. I have compiled the more popular titles for you. I think your sons will find much of the readings from on lists exciting and thought provoking. I've also included a list of favorite children's books for parents of younger children.

Favorite Teenage Books

Author	Title	Copyright	Publisher
Andrews, V. C.	Series of Books		
Atwood, Margaret	*The Handmaid's Tale*	1998	Vintage Anchor
Bach, Richard	*Jonathan Livingston Seagull*	1973	Mass Market Paperback
Blume, Judy	*Are You There God? It's Me Margaret*	1970	Simon & Schuster Children's
Blume, Judy	*Blubber*	1976	Bantam Doubleday Dell Books
Brown, Claude	*Manchild in the Promised Land*	1999	Simon & Schuster
Bryant, Bonnie	*The Horse Whisperer*	1998	Bantam Books
Burnford, Shelia	*The Incredible Journey*	1996	Bantam Doubleday Dell Books for Young Readers
Carmichael, Stokely S., with Charles V. Hamilton	*Black Power*	1976	Vintage Books
Chopin, Kate	*The Awakening*	1981	Bantam Books
Crane, Stephen	*Red Badge of Courage*	1990	Tom Doherty
Dickens, Charles	*Great Expectations*	1990	Doubleday Dell
Downing Hahn, Mary	*Daphne's Book*	1983	Bantam Skylark Books

continued

Author	Title	Copyright	Publisher
Fanon, Franz	White Skin Black Mask	1976	Grove/Atlantic
Haley, Alex	Malcolm "X"	1975	Random House
James, George G. M.	Stolen Legacy	1997	Yale University Press
Keene, Carolyn	The Bungalow Mystery	1960	Gross & Dunlap
King, Stephen	The Stand	1978	Doubleday
Konigsburg, E. L.	From the Mixed-up Files of Mrs. Basil E. Frankweiler	1967	Simon & Schuster
Lamb, Wally	She's Come Undone	1998	Pocket Books
Lee, Harper	To Kill a Mockingbird	1988	Warner Books
Lowry, Lois	The Giver	1994	Houghton Mifflin
Martin, Ann M.	The Baby-sitters Club	1986	Scholastic
Miller, Arthur	The Crucible	1952	Dramatists Play Service
Mitchell, Margaret	Gone with the Wind	1936	McMillan
O'Brien, Tim	The Things They Carried	1998	Random House
Paterson, Katherine	Bridge to Terabithia	1977	HarperCollins
Paulsen, Gary	Hatchet	1987	Penguin Group
Petersen Haddix, Margaret	Among the Hidden	2000	Simon & Schuster
Quinlen, Anna	Black and Blue	1998	Random House
Rand, Ayn	Atlas Shrugged	1996	Mass Market Paperback
Rand, Ayn	The Fountainhead	1952	Signet (Penguin Books)
Rawls, Wilson	Where the Red Fern Grows	1961	Bantam Books
Rockwell, Thomas	How to Eat Fried Worms	1973	Franklin Watts
Sachar, Louis	Holes	1999	Scholastic
Salinger, J. D.	Catcher in the Rye	1991	Little, Brown
Shelley, Mary	Frankenstein	1994	W.W. Norton
Simon, Neil	Biloxi Blues	1986	Random House
Skene Catling, Patrick	The Chocolate Touch	1976	Bantam Book
Spinelli, Jerry	Maniac Magee	1991	HarperCollins
Spinelli, Jerry	Wringer	1997	HarperCollins
Steinbeck, John	Of Mice and Men	1937	Bantam Book
Steinbeck, John	The Pearl	1968	The Viking Press
Taylor, Mildred D.	Roll of Thunder, Hear My Cry	1976	Dial Books
Uris, Leon	Exodus	1958	Doubleday
Wiesel, Elie	Night	1982	Bantam Doubleday Dell

CHAPTER 1: Listen to one Brandenburg Concerto per day
CHAPTER 2: Read a Shakespeare classic to her weekly
CHAPTER 3: Practice creative problem solving three times per week
CHAPTER 4: Do Odyssey of the Mind questions regularly
CHAPTER 5: Memorize all the Math Olympiad higher-level problems
CHAPTER 6: Now what do I do? She's six years above grade level and doing kindergarten work!

TITLE: Giving Birth to a Gifted Baby by P.R.C.

Favorite Children's Books

Author	Title	Copyright	Publisher
Adler, David A.	Cam Jansen and the Missing Cookie	1996	Viking
Berenstain, Stan and Jan	All of the Bernstain Bears books	1980s	Random House
Blume, Judy	Are You There, God? It's Me Margaret	1971	Bantam Doubleday Dell
Blume, Judy	Superfudge	1977	Harcourt Brace
Brittain, Bill	All the Money in the World	1979	Harper Row Junior Books
Burnford, Shelia	The Incredible Journey	1996	Laureleaf
Burton, Virginia Lee	Mike Mulligan and His Steam Shovel	1939	Houghton Mifflin
Caswell, Brian	A Cage of Butterflies	1992	University of Queensland Press
Craighead George, Jean	Julie of the Wolves	1987	HarperCollins Juvenile Books
Cutts & Silverstein	The House that Jack Built	1979	Troll
Dahl, Roald	Charlie and the Chocolate Factory	1998	Puffin
Dahl, Roald	The BFG	1982	Penguin Group
Dahl Roald,	James and the Giant Peach	1961	Penguin Books
Dann, Max	Ernest Pickles Remarkable Robot	1984	Oxford University Press
Dr. Seuss	The Cat in the Hat	1976	Random House
Dr. Seuss	The Lorax	1976	Random House
Erdrich, Louise	The Birchbark House	1999	Hyperion Press

continued

Author	Title	Copyright	Publisher
Fitzgerald, John D.	The Great Brain	1972	Yearling Books
Fitzhugh, Louise	Harriet the Spy	2000	Bantam
Fox, Mem	Wilfred Gordon McDonald Partridge	1984	Kane/Miller
George Speare, Elizabeth	The Witch of Blackbird Pond	1958	Houghton Mifflin
Gramatky, Hardie	Little Toot	1939	G. P. Putnam's Sons
Juster, Norton	The Phantom Tollbooth	1988	Random House
Konigsburg, E. L.	From the Mixed-Up Files of Mrs. Basil E. Frankweiler	1970	Atheneum
Le Tord, BiJou	A Blue Butterfly; A Story about Claude Monet	1995	Delacorte Press
L'Engle, Madeleine	A Wrinkle in Time	1962	Farrar Straus & Giroux
Littledale, Freya	The Magic Fish	1966/1985	Scholastic
Lobel, Arnold	Frog and Toad Are Friends	1970	Harper & Row
Lobel, Arnold	Frog and Toad Together	1979	HarperCollins Children's Books
London, Jack	Call of the Wild	1990	Tor Books
Manus Pinkwater, Daniel	5 Novels: Alan Mendelson the Boy from Mars, Slaves of Speigel, The Snarkout Boys and the Avocado of Deathe, The Last Guru	1997	Farrar Straus & Giroux
Mayer, Mercer	Just Grandma and Me	1983	Golden Books
Munsch, Robert N. and Michael	The Paper Bag Princess	1985	Firefly Books
Norton, Mary	The Borrowers	1998	Harcourt Brace
O'Brien, Robert C.	Mrs. Frisby and the Rats of NIMH	1974	Atheneum
O'Dell, Scott	Island of the Blue Dolphins	1990	Houghton Mifflin
Ottley, Ted	Code of Deception	1993	Random House, Australia
Paulsen, Gary	M.C. Higgins, the Great	1999	Simon & Schuster
Paulsen, Gary	Hachet	1999	Aladdin
Pullman, Philip	The Golden Compass His Dark Materials, No. 1	1996	Knopf
Rawls, Wilson	Where the Red Fern Grows	1961	Curtis
Reid Banks, Lynne	The Indian in the Cupboard	1982	William Morrow

Favorite Children's Books (continued)

Author	Title	Copyright	Publisher
Rowling, J. K.	*Harry Potter and the Goblet of Fire*	2000	Scholastic Press
Rowling, J. K.	*Harry Potter and the Sorcerer's Stone*	1998	Scholastic Trade
Sachar, Louis	*Holes*	1998	Farrar Straus & Giroux
Selden, George	*The Cricket in Times Square*	1983	Farrar Straus & Giroux
Shannon, David	*A Bad Case of the Stripes*	1988	Blue Sky Press
Steig, William	*Dominic*	1984	Farrar Straus & Giroux
Taylor, Mildred D.	*Roll of Thunder, Hear My Cry*	1997	Puffin
Tolan, Stephanie S.	*Welcome to the Ark*	1996	Morrow
Van Allsburg, Chris	*The Polar Express*	1985	Scholastic
White, E. B.	*Charlotte's Web*	1987	HarperCollins
Williams, Margery	*Velveteen Rabbit*	1922/1991	Delcorte Press
Wise Brown, Margaret	*Goodnight Moon*	1947/1975	Harper & Row

3

PERFECTIONISM AND SOCIAL
EMOTIONAL DEVELOPMENT

I am a recovering perfectionist. It's true. I can laugh saying it now, but I spent a great many of my younger years suffering with the pain of perfectionism, and it was painful!

I can clearly remember the Sunday I was playing Toccata and Fugue in F Minor. I was twelve years old and organist at the First Presbyterian Church in Medina, New York. I made a chord mistake and spent the afternoon crying on my bed because I was such a failure in my own mind and heart. Every single week, I prepared the organ music for the Sunday services. All this was done between the ages of twelve and eighteen. Can you imagine? I thought I was a failure because I would make an occasional playing error. Now I wonder how I could even assume that much responsibility at such a young and vulnerable age.

Gifted children often have the talents and responsibilities to assume more adult roles. They are often multipotential. These precious youngsters need guidance with perfectionism, making choices, and managing their time.

Q. Can you explain to me just who perfectionists are?
A. Sure. Generally, perfectionists are people who are very bright and have succeeded because of their high intelligence and many talents. They often can see many solutions to one problem and an infinite number of

ways to solve it. They can create and not feel comfortable with a "finishing point," always knowing more "could be done." Many times, perfectionists will avoid new experiences because of a fear of failure. They're afraid others will view them as inadequate.

Perfectionists have exceedingly high expectations—for themselves and others. On a personal level, these can lead to a workaholic syndrome. On a social level, personality conflicts can ensue at work and at home.

Children can learn perfectionism from their parents and their interactions with them. Such children measure parental acceptance by their perfect deeds and avoid areas where mistakes might be made and a loss of love might occur.

With proper counseling, perfectionists can be helped to lead a more balanced and realistic lifestyle. I'm not sure there is a complete cure for perfectionism, but recovery is possible.

Q. Most parents would probably want this problem, but I'm not sure it's healthy. Our eleven-year-old gifted son is a straight-A student, top in

his class academically, involved on the soccer team, and plays first chair violin in the orchestra. The problem is, Jonathan is so conscientious, he studies or practices all the time, to the exclusion of joining us on family outings, picnics, sports games, or any other form of entertainment. We're very proud of his accomplishments, but somehow, I just don't think this behavior is normal nor healthy. Is it?

A. You're right on one count, not on the other. This behavior is normal for a severe perfectionist and can lead to serious emotional or physical consequences if allowed to continue over a long period of time. You're quite right that this behavior is not healthy.

You can and need to start intervening to help Jonathan with the following steps:

1. Use the time-management sheets at the end of chapter 4 (Time Management, Homework Issues, and S-R-S). Plan times throughout the week and month that your son will join with you in family events. The type and choice of outing can be his, allowing freedom and flexibility. This can certainly include watching some favorite TV shows, seeing movies together, or having a quiet reading time.
2. Plan regular times to sit and talk with Jonathan. Gifted children have a multitude of ideas and thoughts going on in their heads and they benefit greatly by talking. It helps them keep a stable and normal balance.
3. Either utilize the services of your school's counselor or a private one of your choice for Jonathan to speak with. Many times, a child is much more likely to speak with a trusted professional than with a family member or favorite teacher.
4. Walk together. Walking is a wonderful stress-reducer, helps build up natural endorphins in the brain, and a super jibber-jabber time. Once you get your son beyond the initial resistance to the idea, he'll actually look forward to the time together.
5. Always let your son know you care about him. Phrases of endearment and daily hugs or touches provide an immediate and important strength and balance to one's day.

Try any or all of these suggestions. I would be very surprised if you didn't notice improvement after just one or two weeks. If not, e-mail me at szulgit2@aol.com for additional activities.

Q. Our gifted thirteen-year-old daughter is so conscientious and focused on achieving straight As in school, we can't even get her to join us on family outings nor any other social situations. We appreciate her determination to succeed in school academically, but is this normal?

A. Yes and no. Yes, for severe perfectionists; no, for balanced and healthy children. I don't mean to scare you, but you do need to intercede now with your daughter's one-sided behavior (academics to the exclusion of social and family activities). The longer this behavior is allowed to go on, the harder it will be to bring your daughter to a more balanced lifestyle. Perfectionism is a painful behavior. Good is never good enough; excellence is never excellent enough. There can be many reasons for her perfectionism.

Regardless of your daughter's reasons, it is interfering with her social and family life and counseling now would help her a great deal. One option is counseling within school, although this is many times embarrassing to the children amongst their peers. Unfortunately, often the school counselor's (or psychologist's) time is overloaded with the low-achieving and discipline students.

There might be subsidized family counseling centers through your local township or hospitals.

Private psychologists and counselors could be costly, but are often covered by medical health insurance companies.

Check with your daughter's teachers or call your school psychologist to find the names of the professionals who specialize in gifted children or severe perfectionists. The sooner you start on this road, the better.

Q. Why are some students "workaholics?"

A. The "healthy" reason is that these children want to succeed, produce excellence in their work while keeping up with the homework demands of their schools and teachers . . . all honorable goals.

However, all too often, workaholic children are that way due to a variety of factors that do not constitute a balanced, healthy emotional lifestyle. Children most at risk for becoming workaholics are those between the ages of six and twelve who have repeatedly been rewarded only for the things they do rather than for the personal qualities they have.

Many times, these children have parents who push them to extreme limits and are very dominant in their children's development. Such parents often are trying to live and succeed through their gifted children. More often than not, these children "burn out" as adults and never even come close to achieving their true potential.

Perfectionism and its many roles, also plays a very strong factor in producing severe workaholics. Adderholdt and Goldberg (1999, 18–21)[1] aptly describe the eight games perfectionists play, believing that achievement and self-worth are one and the same:

- *Riding the Mood Roller Coaster:* You set a goal for yourself (for example, to ace a math test). You do it—and you feel great! But you don't ace the next one—you get an 89. And you feel awful. Your friends and family notice and try to reassure you, but you're prickly and irritable and suspicious of their motives. Why would they praise you? You're not worth it; you couldn't even get that A you were after! Then along comes the next math test, you ace it, and you're riding high again. It's exhausting! You feel excited and capable when you do well, and unacceptable and ashamed when you don't.

---

[1] Excerpted from *Perfectionism: What's Bad about Being Too Good?* (*Revised and Updated Edition*) by Miriam Adderholdt and Jan Goldberg © 1999. Used with permission from Free Spirit Publishing, Inc., Minneapolis, Minn.; 1-800-735-7323; www.freespirit.com. All rights reserved.

- *The Numbers Game:* The quantity of achievements or actions becomes more important than the quality. You start to focus on how many trophies you win, papers you write, awards you receive, honors you reap—not what you're learning or what they're really worth. No number is ever high enough; you just keep counting.
- *Focusing on the Future:* You give an especially brilliant speech during the debate. Everybody comes up afterward and tells you that you were inspiring. But all you can think about is what you forgot to say. Or your mind is already on next week's essay contest—what if you don't outdo yourself in that, too? Don't even try to sit back and savor your success; that's not what perfectionists do. There's no time, not when you're already planning the future and worrying about the things you must do to succeed.
- *Pining over the Past:* "If only I'd . . ." "Why didn't I . . ." "This wouldn't have happened if I'd started sooner." "If I'd put down that answer, I would've got an A instead of a B." You don't let things go. You chew on them relentlessly, like a dog gnawing on a bone. Thoughts like these keep you stuck in the same old groove of the same old record.
- *Telescopic Thinking:* You use both ends of a telescope when viewing your achievements. When looking at the goals you haven't met, you use the magnifying end so they appear much larger than they really are. But when looking at those you have met, you use the "minifying" end so they appear minute and insignificant. For example, you win the district tennis match, but you can't feel good about it because you haven't won the state. Or you compete in the state tournament, making it all the way to the championship match, but feel outclassed the minute your opponent pulls ahead.
- *Putting Your Goals First:* Given a choice between sleeping and studying, you study—even if it means drinking gallons of coffee or taking caffeine pills, pinching yourself to stay awake, and making yourself sick. Or given the choice between going out with friends or working on your volleyball serve, you opt for the gym. Your achievement goals always come before fun or friends or your own good health.
- *Getting It Right:* You're not satisfied with anything but the best, most perfect results, so you do the same thing again . . . and again . . . and again until you get it right. Maybe you repeat the same course in

school until you get the A you're determined to have. Or you play the same piece of music over and over and over and over and over and over and over and over and over and over and over again, hating yourself because you're so slow. You're worried that others will know how hard you worked when you want it to appear effortless.

- *All-or-Nothing Thinking:* You're not satisfied unless you have it all—all the track trophies, all the academic awards your school can give, all the leadership positions in your clubs. One B or one second place is enough to tip you over into the feeling that you've failed, that you're not good enough.

As school counselors and educators become more aware of perfectionism and how it adversely affects so many of our gifted children, proactive counseling classes and interventions will hopefully become a more standard part of our children's days.

Q. Year after year after year, teachers and counselors have told my husband and me that our son is an underachiever, yet none of the teachers have been able to get him to "achieve" at their "expected levels" for him. He maintains a B average, plays sports, and seems pretty content to us. Should we be expecting more of him? We want our son to be happy, healthy, and psychologically adjusted. Are we letting him "waste his potential"?

A. It sounds to me like you're doing just fine in your parenting role. Many perfectionist-gifted children are emotionally devastated if they earn a grade of B yet, by definition, a B represents an achievement that is "very good!"

I do have to wonder if your son is achieving Bs because he already knows the grade-level materials and can breeze right through the assignments and tests. I am also concerned that he might be an underachiever because he is not being educated at his aptitude level, like so many of our gifted children in American schools. If this is the case, I encourage you to meet with your son's teachers and review his achievement and nationally normed scores. If his test scores indicate he has been or is achieving one, two, or even more years ahead of his peers and grade-level expectations, then I suspect this is why the teachers have been suggesting "underachievement" to you.

Be careful with the solutions suggested. Many times, gifted children are given more work as a challenge and this becomes the "typical punishment" for being bright! Enrichment is also overused to the point that the overload of enrichment activities at grade levels can be seen coming out of the students' ears!

At the elementary level, compacting is an easy solution by testing children through materials they already know and getting them educated at an instructional level compatible to their achievement and aptitude. This is the positive. The negative is, often times high-achieving students are given packets to work on at a higher grade level, but without proper instructions and monitoring. They are often left to sit in the hall outside the room to do their assignments. This is a lonely road to walk for these students and not educationally instructive nor emotionally supportive.

In middle and high schools, accelerated courses or AP courses often serve to educate the gifted and more cognitively advanced students. The positive is that high-achieving students are together and hopefully working at compatible aptitude levels. The negatives could be excessive amounts of homework and in some districts, AP courses are not weighted, so an A in Advanced Calculus is weighted the same as an A in regular Calculus. Cumulative averages remain the same, yet the amount and degree of work vary significantly. Class standings could be affected as well as scholarship awards.

These are ideas to consider when you meet with your son's teachers and review his test scores and patterns of achievement.

If you agree that advancing his studies is an appropriate answer, be sure you include your son in the discussion. Depending on how long he has been underachieving, if this is the case, working at the appropriate aptitude level more than likely is going to be a jolt, both academically and emotionally.

First and foremost, your son's emotional and physical health are important. Right now, it sounds like he's pretty happy and successful according to basic school standards and so are you. Working together with your son and his teachers, I suspect you'll come up with the proper answer.

Q. My nine-year-old son will lie awake for hours each night, unable to fall asleep. Is there anything I can do to help him gain a more peaceful night's sleep? Suggestions, please.

A. When I first started teaching my Parenting the Gifted class at a local university, it rapidly became very clear that many of the parents had

children who could not sleep well. My answer to them was, talk, talk, talk! In fact, I promised that if each parent sat on his child's bed and talked with his child for the next seven nights, there would be no more sleep problems. I promised.

What were they to talk about? Anything! I suggested letting the children lead the conversations. Mrs. P reported her son talked three hours the first night, from 10 P.M. to 1 A.M. She even dozed off in the rocking chair a few times but her son simply awakened her. Progress? . . . yes! By the fifth night, Roger was dozing off to a peaceful sleep after forty-five minutes of talking and Mr. P traded some nights with Mrs. P, so she could have a full night of sleep herself!

Twelve of the fifteen parents reported positive progress with their children's sleep patterns at our next class.

Q. How can I get counseling help at school for my gifted nine-year-old? He has trouble relating to his peers and is a severe perfectionist. The counseling time allotted to our school is being used up by the slower-achieving students, special education students, and troublemakers. We can't afford to pay for outside counseling services.
A. I literally had to fight ten years to get any counseling time whatsoever for the children in my self-contained gifted classroom, and then it was only for thirty minutes a week! Gifted students have unique counseling needs, including social and emotional adjustment, perfectionism, career planning, underachievement, multipotentiality, and family relationships. First, talk to you child's teachers in gaining support for in-school counseling. Second, check your child's group IQ test results and standardized achievement test scores, or you can request an individual WISQ-R by the school psychologist. This score usually runs higher than the group normed tests. This gives you positive "data" as you request a fair and appropriate education for your child, including counseling.

A note from your child's pediatrician requesting testing or counseling is usually beneficial as well.

If all else fails, go to your administration and school board representatives—but always in a positive and supportive role. I know it's very frustrating at times, but keep P and P (Positive and Proactive)!

Q. My teenage daughter seems to be crying at the slightest little happening at home. She argues constantly with her father and me, as well

as with her two younger siblings, and is sleeping much more than usual. Her grades are starting to drop and I'm beginning to seriously worry about her. Could she be depressed or just going through the "struggles" of teenage years? Susan is fifteen years old.

A. Many times, there is a fine line between the symptoms of excessive stress, "teenage turmoil," and depression. There is a clear difference with clinical depression. This needs to be treated by a trained professional. Susan cannot just "will" her way out of clinical depression. The fact that your daughter is sleeping excessively and crying with little provocation suggests to me an immediate visit to her internist. He can provide a proper diagnosis and the necessary medication if Susan is clinically depressed.

If not, Susan still needs help dealing with the events going on in her life. Many of today's gifted children are multipotential and have excessively overloaded schedules and commitments, pursuing excellence in many of their gifted areas.

Multipotential high school children are often involved in AP classes, musical groups, debate clubs, church groups, athletics, community services, and mentorships. This list goes on and on and on! Coupled with an office visit to Susan's internist, please take the time to sit down with her and talk. She may be initially resistant, but after a burst of tears, she may well start blurting out the major cause of her changes in behavior, including being overwhelmed with too many activities. She may also need help with time management and study habits, which I cover in another chapter.

The main thrust here is to get started with an intervention.

Q. What happens to gifted children? Do most succeed as adults?
A. Certainly giftedness is not a sole measure of success in life. There are a variety of variables that can and do affect a gifted child's success as an adult. Overall, I agree with Ellen Winner's (1996) summation[2] of the factors that predict the four possible combinations of "gifted child and adult outcomes":

- Those gifted children most likely to develop their talent to the level of an expert will be those who have high drive and the ability to focus and derive flow from their work, those who grow up in families that combine stimulation with support, and those who are fortunate to have inspiring teachers, mentors, and role models.
- Those gifted children most likely to leave their creative mark on a domain in adulthood will also have high drive, focus, and flow, and inspiring mentors and models. But in two other areas they should be different. They should be willing to be nonconforming, take risks, and shake up the established tradition. And they are generally more likely to have grown up in stressful family conditions. (Although stress may be a facilitating factor, it is surely not sufficient, and is not a factor for parents to strive for!) Many are also likely to develop some form of affective disorder. In addition, they must be born when the times are right: their domains must be ready for the kinds of changes they envision, and there must not be too many others likely to beat them in revolutionizing the domain first.
- Those gifted children predicted to burn out are those whose parents push them to extremes and are overinvolved in their development. These parents differ from those who produce creative children. Parents of future creators cause stress in their children's lives, but they are not overinvolved. Instead, they encourage independence in their offspring. But the difficulty of prediction is brought home by

---

[2] Excerpted from *Gifted Children: Myths and Realities* by Ellen Winner. Copyright © 1996 by Ellen Winner. Reprinted by permission of Basic Books, a member of Perseus Books, L.L.C.

the fact that John Stuart Mill, who was excessively pushed by his father, did not drop out, whereas William James Sidis did.

- Those gifted children not "born into" a domain often discover their ultimate calling in adulthood when they are catalyzed by a crystallizing experience, a life-changing event in which a gift is discovered and self-doubts are dispelled.

I, personally, have always fallen into the category of "should be willing to be nonconforming, take risks, and shake up the established tradition!" This was never a conscious decision nor easy path to follow. I was always personally and professionally true to myself and my ideals. It seemed to me to be the only way to go!

I have become increasingly aware of the need to support, guide, and direct our nonconforming, risk-taking gifted children, teaching them strategies and the politics of how to challenge the establishment successfully. Why get your head chopped off if you can walk away with change and only a few bruises here and there?

Q. Can you recommend any books for my thirteen-year-old child to read? He is a severe perfectionist and no matter how hard I try to help him "balance" his activities, the "perfectionism" always wins!
A. Yes. There are two that I particularly like and have used with my graduate students as well as elementary and middle school children:

Adderholdt, M., and J. Goldberg. *Perfectionism: What's Bad about Being Too Good*? Minneapolis, Minn: Free Spirit Publishing, 1999
Hipp, Earl. *Fighting Invisible Tigers*. Minneapolis, Minn.: Free Spirit Publishing, 1995.

Both of these books deal with the possible underlying causes of perfectionism, suggest ways to recover, and offer a sense of humor while doing so.

4

TIME MANAGEMENT, HOMEWORK ISSUES, AND SCHOOL-RELATED STUDIES (S-R-S)

I have seen the "misuse" of homework become a crushing negative to hundreds of thousands of students of all ability levels over my thirty-four-year educational career.

For example, Eric's Math I teacher would sometimes assign nightly homework of up to 105 problems. First, if Eric already understood the classwork, wouldn't five or six similar problems be enough reinforcement? And if he didn't get the day's lesson, where was the teacher in the evening to help with the comprehension and solutions?

The time alone needed to solve 105 math problems is a crusher for many students, not to mention the time needed to complete other teacher assignments accumulated throughout the day.

I believe homework is the number 1 enemy of gifted children and perhaps all children in our American schools. The entire use of—or rather, misuse of—homework continues to frustrate me as an educator and a parent. If I started listing the horror stories I've seen and heard concerning homework over the years of my career, I still wouldn't be finished writing this book twenty years from now. There are clear-cut answers to avoid this often negative and counterproductive pitfall in the misuse of homework, which I deal with throughout this chapter. Keep reading.

Q. My child has been identified as "gifted," yet the only difference I can see in her school is "more" and "harder" homework. This doesn't seem right to me. Do you agree?

A. Yes, I agree. This is not right. The three classic misuses of gifted children in our educational system are:

1. Use of high-achieving students as tutors for the slower-achieving students.
2. Piling on more enrichment activities at grade-level expectations to keep the gifted students learning or occupied while their slower-achieving classmates work on completing their own assignments.
3. Assigning more and harder work to the gifted students. In effect, this becomes a punishment for being bright.

A great deal of this problem can be eliminated through the use of curriculum compacting and subject integration. Pretesting the achievement levels of the gifted student before teaching and then compacting can save weeks and months of repetitive work. Prescribing appropriate work at their aptitude and achievement levels is a clear key in the education of our gifted children in America. You need to talk with your daughter's teachers now, if not sooner!

Q. Our eight-year-old daughter seems to possess quite a talent on the violin and has been playing/studying with a local violinist in the philharmonic since she was five. Her teacher feels JoEllen has a very promising career. Just one problem . . . all she wants to do is practice the violin to the exclusion of all her other school assignments! We continue to receive notes from her teachers about incompletes or assignments never done. What are we to do? The word "prodigy" has been used in reference to JoEllen.
A. If there is such a thing as a good dilemma, then I believe you have one. This is where your job as a parent begins. JoEllen is unique and uniquely talented:

1. Meet with your school personnel and discuss ways JoEllen's schooling/assignments might be modified to support her musical genius.
2. Set up a time-management sheet for daily, short-term, and long-term assignments with your daughter. I've included a sample at the end of this chapter. Her learning style might be "abstract random," which could make it more difficult for her to focus on a multitude of assignments and manage her time wisely. This is not an uncommon problem.
3. Set aside an agreed amount of time at home after school where JoEllen can work on specific assignments or school-related studies in a quiet, personal space. This will help her focus and reinforce responsibility. The same can be true for violin practicing time and family interactions, such as dinner together.
4. Check to see if the amount of "homework" being given to your fourth grader is fair and necessary.
5. Communicate with your daughter regularly. Many gifted children have a great need to talk. This helps them sort out issues and not make mountains out of molehills.
6. Repeat #1 on a regular basis.

Q. In primary school, our eight-year-old son tested off the charts in both math and reading. What should we do to ensure he receives an appropriate education for his achievement level?

A. When I was the facilitator for gifted and talented (K–8), before I went into full-time consulting, I was assigned to a gifted third grader, who in kindergarten had scored post high school in aptitude and achievement tests. Eric's greatest cognitive gift is in the field of mathematics. He is quite brilliant in this academic arena. Yet his homeroom teacher insisted that he should "clean and organize" his desk like everyone else, and that he shouldn't receive any special privileges. Here we had an eight-year-old whose mathematical aptitude surpassed his peers by at least nine years, if not more. His brain was working at a level beyond most of us, yet keeping his desk in order was one of the priorities of Eric's teacher. This simply was not an easy task for this child and, quite frankly, probably was not a priority in his brain.

I used to go into his classroom twice a week about two hours after the schoolchildren and teacher had gone home and organize Eric's desk for him. You see, I believed this was one of many small ways I could help Eric.

I also met with him weekly and developed a social/emotional trust, worked on issues of perfectionism, and we became mutually respectful friends. These were ways I knew could help him.

I must compliment Eric's school and district in general for developing and adapting a program to educationally serve his cognitive giftedness and social development.

As a second grader, Eric spent forty-five minutes a day in a sixth-grade mathematics class. While trying to close the gap academically, this was an uncomfortable situation socially for Eric, quite understandably. In third grade, the sixth-grade math teacher voluntarily gave up her daily planning time four days a week and was paid tutoring time by the district to work with Eric on mathematics.

As a fourth grader, his parents drove him to the middle school, where Eric took Math I first period with eighth and ninth graders. He scored 96 percent on the New York State Regents. And on the successful story goes . . . a 100 percent on Math II Regents and just this past year, Eric was on the TV special *America's Genius: Level II*, where he made it through to the semifinal round, winning a $25,000 college trust fund, a trip for four to Hawaii, a 68" color TV, a Palm computer, and an all-expenses paid trip for himself and his family to and from Los Angeles.

I've mentioned all this to you because JoEllen and Eric are unique, prodigies if you will. Eric did not clean and organize his desk. JoEllen did not always complete assignments. As parents and educators we can help these and other children manage time, set priorities, and achieve a balanced and healthy life for themselves.

We can also work with our children's schools to help in the development of their appropriate and adequate education. There are models that do exist.

Q. What's the proper amount of after-school and weekend activities I should have my child involved in?

A. Many gifted children are multipotential. They have the ability and desire to do unlimited amounts of cognitive, social, and athletic activities. In theory, this is wonderful! In practice, it can be less than positive.

I've always been a huge proponent for creative thinking and emotional/physical relaxation. I would occasionally give only one "homework assignment" for an evening to my elementary and middle school students. This was in my pre "school-related studies" (S-R-S) days. It would be to go to their bedrooms for thirty minutes, shut their doors, and lie down on their beds and relax.

Their initial reactions were almost comical. "Dr. C, what do you want us to do while we lie there? What should we think about? What if we fall asleep? Can I read? Can I talk to my friends on the phone? What if I can't stay in one place that long?"

To me, these questions were a clear indication that our children are overextended and, more important, they haven't been taught or slowed down enough to think for themselves and relax.

I simply responded by saying, "Your only assignment is to go in your bedroom for thirty minutes, shut the door, and lie down on your bed. Cover up with a cozy blanket if you want."

Regardless of the grade or age level I tried this with, the results were almost uniform.

Some children slept for well more than a half hour. Others thought about their friends and family relationships—good features, as well as areas that needed improvement(s).

Still others read a book they personally enjoyed rather than an assigned book or a specified amount of pages/chapters. One sixth grader read for five hours and "polished off" the Newbery book *Maniac Magee.* Wow, what a concept—reading for pleasure—an art form we're losing because we are overloading our children with preassigned homework and assigned readings every day and weekend.

When we'd have a school holiday, I'd ask the children to take just one hour of that day and pick an S-R-S activity of their choice. I told them I would do the same.

Bedrooms were organized, students caught up on assignments, a majority read books of their choice, and others developed their own Web pages or worked on the computer.

My overriding suggestion to you is to ensure your child has time during the week to reflect, rest, do assignments, catch up on assignments, eat dinner with the family, talk, and not be out of the house every afternoon or night.

You'll definitely know your child is overinvolved if she is cranky, overtired, stressed, not finishing assignments, or doing projects/assignments without quality, instead, racing to get things done.

Balance is such an important concept in our mental, physical, family, social, and academic health. We owe it to our children to help them manage time and to select and achieve balance in their lives.

Q. I'm at my wits' end. My fifteen-year-old gifted child is an extreme procrastinator and consequently, his grades suffer due to assignments turned in late. Can you please help?
A. Yes, I can, and this "homework hazard" is not uncommon for gifted students—and adults! Many of us like to work under "last-minute stress," but this is different from perfectionists who avoid getting started, due to fear of failure and procrastination.

You will be an enormous help to your son by sitting down with him and talking through the approximate amounts of time he'll need for his daily, short-term, and long-term assignments. Then be sure he has a

Five Tips for Procrastinators

1. Plot out your daily, short-term, and long-term assignments on the monthly time-management sheet I've included at the end of this chapter. Seeing the actual schedule makes the workload far less intimidating and much easier to tackle.
2. Find a quiet room in your house that you can claim at any time for your studying purposes. Try to keep it organized!
3. Set aside one hour every weekend to clean your bedroom, organize your thoughts, and look over your upcoming assignments for the next week. This helps you focus and calm down!
4. Look over the coming week's TV shows and specials in your local TV guide. Allow yourself a half hour or hour a day where you can relax and unwind and catch up on your favorite shows. Looking forward to this treat keeps you motivated on your study tasks.
5. Plan out a tentative time of day, afternoon, or evening when you will work on your school assignments and other commitments each day. Discuss this with your parents so they can support you and help other family members (siblings) respect your quiet study time. Be flexible. A large block of time on Saturdays (two hours) can help avoid the Sunday evening panic and shortage of time.

quiet place to study and enforce an agreed amount of time for his daily studies at home.

If your son is involved with musical activities, sports, or school clubs, you need to think about whether or not he is overextended. There are only so many hours in a day and week, and he needs a balance between work and play.

Q. My son is always leaving his assignments (work) until the very last minute. Then he panics, gets the entire house in an uproar (emotionally and physically), and many times winds staying up the entire night before the project is due. I'm at my wits' end and don't know how to help. Please advise!!!!

A. You can very definitely help your son by sitting down with him and plotting out on a calendar when his long-term and short-tem projects and assignments are due. Then you need to pick a mutually agreeable time with him when he'll do his work at home each day . . . no excuses. Many times, the hardest part of doing a project or assignment is getting started. Having an assigned time to study/work at home each day is the best way to help your child get started and avoid these last-minute panics and family disruptions. I've included an example of a monthly time-management calendar at the end of this chapter for you.

SCHOOL-RELATED STUDIES:

A KEY TO SUCCESS

SCHOOL-RELATED STUDIES (S-R-S)

I developed school-related studies (S-R-S) fifteen years ago to help students and parents relate to learning as an ongoing process occurring naturally, linking their school daytime and thinking with their evening at home. Its goal was to reinforce, extend, and enrich learning presented in school. It has worked equally successfully with first graders, fourth graders, middle schoolers, and every age in between.

Grade	Minutes
Kindergarten	20 minutes
1st Grade	25 minutes
2nd Grade	30 minutes
3rd Grade	35 minutes
4th Grade	40 minutes
5th Grade	50–60 minutes
6th Grade	60–75 minutes

For a majority of students, the issue of homework had become a negative force rather than the positive educational practice it was originally intended to be, a practice or reinforcement of newly studied objectives. This truly hurt my heart, as learning can be a joyful gift in life. Thus, I invented S-R-S!

School-related studies is intended to

- Foster a love of learning in all students,
- Promote ongoing learning outside the school setting,
- Improve students' independent work habits,
- Strengthen the communication between home and school,
- Raise standards and improve academic performance, and
- Address individual interests and needs of students at all academic levels.

I expected a minimum designated time period to be maintained after school for school-related studies by all of my students five or six days out of each week. Parents agreed to help their children select a quiet, well-lighted area where their children could attend to their S-R-S. They also helped their children make good decisions as they related to their choice of activities. This provided a pleasant, cooperative family planning time together.

During S-R-S students usually prioritize their work as follows:

1. Complete any unfinished classwork or assignments due the very next day if not completed in allotted time at school.
2. Study for upcoming tests, work on long-term projects, or review work covered in class.
3. Choose something related to thinking/school topics that supported academic interests/needs. This could include reading a book of choice, visiting the library, organizing their bedroom, writing a thank-you note, visiting a town board meeting for government,

studying for Math Olympiads, working on an art project, or Odyssey of the Mind project, to mention just a few.

Suggested daily minimum time arrangement, per grade level, are shown in the chart on page 60.

School-related studies definitely empowered parents as prime supporters of their children's focused and daily quiet study times at home. It also helped the children focus on daily and long-term assignments. Gone were the daily exchanges between parent and child:

"Hi, Johnny. How was your day at school today?"

"O.K., mom."

"Any homework tonight?"

"No, mom."

Ha! Ha! Home and school become linked with united and similar expectations.

The biggest and most positive change I noticed after the initial transition period into S-R-S was a significant increase in the amount of pleasure reading my students were doing.

This was true across grade levels. My intermediate students and middle schoolers were polishing off Newbery books and other novels they loved in two or three days. In fact, at least one-third of my students significantly increased their S-R-S time voluntarily! Indeed, learning and reading were becoming pleasurable again!

The same was true for my primary students. Reading time increased two-, three-, and fourfold.

Of equal importance along with positive increases in "attitude toward learning" with S-R-S were the increases in test scores and subsequent increases in self-concept of my students. As part of school-related studies, I required a minimum of 20 percent of S-R-S to be used three days in a row to study for an upcoming major test. This helped kids get away from cramming the night before a test, helped keep learning from being a last-minute review process, and oftentimes helped parents become involved with their child in studying for tests.

Enjoyment in learning, increasing test scores, increasing positive self-concept, strengthened home/school connection and communication, reading for pleasure, applicable leanings, etc.—wow, what more could we ask for in a positive and successful school environment?

Bravo for S-R-S!!!!

Why "S-R-S."?

- Addresses individual needs of students at all academic levels
- Help improve students' independent work habits
- Teach students "how to learn" by utilizing skills such as time management, organization, and good study habits

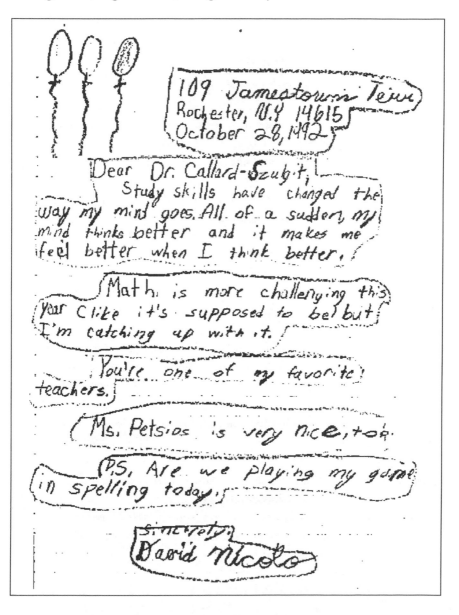

School-Related Studies

- *Reinforce*
- *Extend*
- *Enrich*

Concepts Presented in Classes

SQ3R

Survey:	Look over the entire book, chapter, or whatever contents you're going to read. This should include table of contents, appendices, author's notes, etc.
Question:	Go over the questions at the end of the chapter or devise your own based on what you viewed during your survey. This is especially good for directed reading/study goals and helps keep you focused.
Read:	Begin reading with your questions actively in your mind. When you find an answer, highlight it or make a * nearby.
Recall/Recite:	Try and recite the important information, definitions, and answers to questions from the material you just read. If you can, bravo. If not, focus, re-read the parts you need to and try again. This is an important step that solidifies the materials in your brain and makes reviewing for tests much easier.
Review:	This can be done in a variety of ways: discussing the material with someone else, checking margin notes, highlighted materials and underlined sections, or quickly re-reading. Repeated review helps store knowledge in your long-term memory.

Adapted from Mind Tools: http//www.mindtools.com/sq3r.html.

SQ3R

A time-tested and very successful studying technique is SQ3R, involving the surveying, questioning, reading, reciting, and reviewing of materials. Go over this method with your child and help him get into the habit of using it to study.

I used SQ3R regularly with my students and it made an amazing difference in their comprehension and achievement test scores!

TIME-MANAGEMENT SHEET

Month of: _____

Name: _____

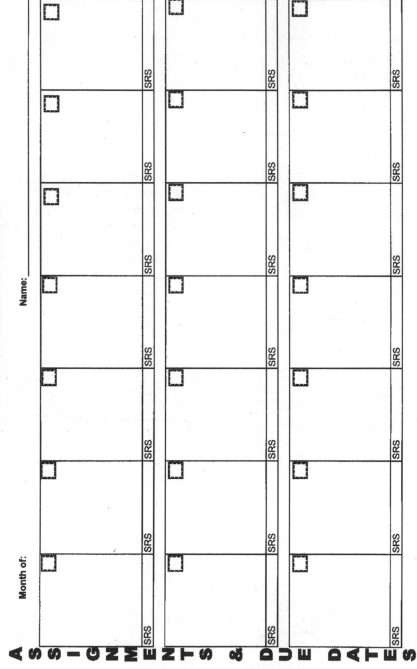

TIME-MANAGEMENT SHEET

ASSIGNMENTS & DUE DATES

Month of: _____   Name: _____

☐	☐	☐	☐	☐	☐	☐
SRS	SRS	SRS	SRS	SRS	SRS	SRS

☐	☐	☐	☐	☐	☐	☐
SRS	SRS	SRS	SRS	SRS	SRS	SRS

☐	☐	☐	☐ NOTES:
SRS	SRS	SRS	

JUST SAY

NO

TO
PROCRASTINATION!

5

ADVOCACY

One of my very favorite stories I use in advocacy training, which re-flects an educational environment and value system in support (or not) of programming in a school district for gifted, is the *Palcuzzi Ploy* (Gallagher and Gallagher 1994, 91–92).

THE PALCUZZI PLOY

Mr. Palcuzzi, principal of the Jefferson Elementary School, got tired of hearing objections to special provisions for gifted children, so he de-cided to spice up an otherwise mild PTA meeting with *his* proposal for gifted children.

The elements of the Palcuzzi program were as follows:

1. Children should be grouped by ability.
2. Part of the school day should be given over to special instruction.
3. Talented students should be allowed time to share their talents with children of other schools in the area or even of other schools throughout the state. (We will pay the transportation costs.)

4. Children should be advanced according to their talents, rather than their age.
5. These children should have specially trained and highly salaried teachers.

As might be expected, the Palcuzzi program was subjected to a barrage of criticism: "What about the youngsters who aren't able to fit into the special group, won't their egos be damaged?" "How about the special cost? How could you justify transportation costs that would have to be paid by moving a special group of students from one school to another?" "Won't we be endangering the children by having them interact with others who are much more mature?" "Wouldn't the other teachers complain if we gave more money to the instructors of this group?"

After listening for ten or fifteen minutes, Palcuzzi dropped his bomb. He said that he was not describing a *new* program for the intellectually gifted, but a program the school system had been enthusiastically supporting for a number of years—the program for *gifted basketball players*! Palcuzzi took advantage of the silence that followed to review his program again.

The irony this story portrays is that if a school community likes, values, and enjoys a program, protests can be nonexistent.

If the community does not value or support a gifted program, all sorts of protests are voiced! Sad, but true.

Q. What are my rights as a parent of a gifted child?
A. Your rights as a parent of a gifted child are the same as all other parents.

- Your have the right to be your child's #1 advocate.
- You have the right to a fair and equitable education for your child.
- You have the right to know when local standardized tests are being given and see sample tests with question and answers.
- You have the right to join your local and state PTA and advocate for the understanding, training, and support of gifted children with programming for the gifted.
- As a member of your school and district PTA, you have the right to expect those organizations to schedule speakers who are experts in the field of gifted education.

- You have the right to know all of your child's test scores and what they mean.
- You have the right to study sessions where differentiated curriculums and classrooms with compacted curriculums are explained to you.
- You have the right to expect your child's teacher to love, respect, and educate your child with the same amount of time and dedication he gives to all the other children in the classroom.
- You have the right to feel comfortable and supported by the educational system as a parent and advocate for your child, gifted children, and all children.

Q. How can I be the best advocate possible for my child?

A. Know that as you work in school groups, community organizations, and neighborhood activities, there will most likely be a prejudice against the "gifted." I even found this throughout my career from many of my fellow educators and administrators. Terms such as "elitist" or "egotistical" are often levied in arguments against providing appropriate programs and activities for children identified as gifted. Unfortunately, this is often because of a lack of understanding of who qualifies and what we mean by the term *gifted*. Many teachers are still not being educated in differentiating and compacting curriculums, which work for all kids— not just gifted.

Consequently, it's important for you to do your "homework" and familiarize yourself with the definitions and appropriate programming models and curriculum options.

Stay positive as you help other parents and teachers understand this often-misunderstood field. Write your local, state, and national political leaders requesting their help in allocating funds and resources for the gifted.

Join your local and state advocacy groups. On the national level, the National Association for Gifted Children (NAGC) provides conferences, publications, and current research about gifted education.

As a stepparent of four gifted children and educator advocate my entire career for the rights of all children, including gifted, I can tell you, advocacy will be a constant uphill journey. I know you can do it! I did! Read on for my suggested steps to follow.

Q. Our daughter, Sally, has an early birthday and could start school this September. This would make her the youngest, or one of the youngest, in her class throughout her thirteen-year school career. She is a very precocious and started reading at the age of three. I'm torn between starting her in school with all its activities and advantages and knowing she'll always be younger than her classmates. I want to do what's socially, emotionally, and intellectually best for our daughter. What do you suggest?
A. I've done a complete about-face on this very same issue since my career began. In my opinion, all the advantages weigh in on the side of your daughter being one of the oldest rather than one of the youngest in her class. Physically, she'll be more developed, emotionally, she'll have experienced more. She'll have had the advantage intellectually of more environmental influences and cognitive experiences over time.

There are so many games and educational materials available to parents and the general public now, I encourage you to spend quality family time utilizing these with your daughter this next year before entering her into kindergarten. Frequent visits to the public library, overnights with neighborhood children, peaceful times to create and think on her own at home without the pressures of constant homework—she'll never receive these to the same extent again, once Sally starts her public school career.

Another important point to consider is the extent to which your school district services its precocious and gifted children. You need to start asking questions and doing some research into the district's policy toward gifted children. If Sally is going to do the same things in kindergarten she already knows how to do at home, by all means, do *not* start her school career early. Take full advantage of that extra year at home.

Q. How are we supposed to know what the "proper" amount of parental discipline is? My husband and I feel very strongly that our children should do their schoolwork, do it well, then "play" all they want. Most of the other parents in our neighborhood are very lax with their children, saying they want their children to have fun and enjoy life! What is fair?

A. Parents are the #1 advocates for their children and therefore assume a prominent role in the home setting for rules, expectations for success, and quality of work. They are also role models for peer relationships as well as independent learning outside of work and school.

Creating an atmosphere where your children can be free to develop their own unique and creative talents is essential to their positive mental health. Too much freedom can foster underachievement and an inability to set realistic goals, including time needed to complete short- and long-term assignments.

Many elementary and middle school children need help with time management. As a teacher and parent, I believe it is of the utmost importance for you and your husband to set clear parameters as to when and how much time your children should be spending each day on schoolwork and other responsibilities. Whenever possible, have your family eat together. This time provides a wonderful outlet for intellectual thinking, discussions, family closeness, and reflection time with each other.

If your children want "down time" when they first arrive home from school, I totally support this. Our brains and bodies need peaceful times to relax, reflect, create, and renew—children as well as adults.

From my experience as an educator, I believe there are maximum amounts of time children at various ages should have to spend daily on homework. Please refer to chapter 4. If these times are exceeded on a regular basis, your school's policy on homework needs to be questioned and evaluated.

Discuss and evaluate your rules and study expectations regularly with your children. Include them in the decisions. Compromise can be a very productive win-win situation for you and your children.

You and your husband are the adults in your family, with wisdom and experience on your side. Your children count on you to provide a safe and structured home environment for them. As long as you're fair and realistic, your children will forever be grateful to you for your discipline and caring.

Q. We have moved three times during our children's school educations. Both our children, ten and thirteen years old, have been identified as gifted, yet the services provided (or not) from school district to school district vary significantly. How can we meet with our children's current district, asking for an appropriate education, referencing current standards, and not alienate the teachers?

A. I understand your plight and empathize with you, your children, and your children's teachers. During the past decade, significant numbers of gifted programs have been dropped in districts, some due to budget cuts and others due to the controversy and misunderstandings surrounding gifted programs. The special education inclusion model has been sweeping the country, giving equal access in heterogeneously grouped classrooms to identified special education students and remedial students. A special education teacher "pushes in" to help the regular classroom teacher with the extra classroom numbers, workload, and classroom management, but who is there to help differentiate and cognitively challenge the gifted?

There are some basic steps and information gathering I encourage you to do before the meeting with your children's teachers in your new school district.

- Talk with other parents in your neighborhood, church, or athletic club, anywhere you can find them, asking what they particularly like about their children's schooling, including teachers, class sizes, intellectual clubs, community service organizations, fitness programs, and social activities. Of particular interest to you would be the district's attitude and programming service for gifted children.
- Find out if the rights of gifted children and gifted education programs are protected by law in your state. Currently, about 50 percent of the states legally protect the right to an appropriate education for their gifted children.
- Question your children regularly on what they especially enjoy and don't enjoy about school. Are they learning new things or studying lessons and materials they already know? Is a part of every day being used by them to tutor or help slower-learning or remedial students? If they finish assignments early, are they required to then go to one of the learning centers in their room or are they given choices?
- Is the curriculum differentiated for them, or are they given more and harder work?
- Have an idea in mind as to what changes or challenges would benefit your children before meeting with their teachers. Change almost always comes slowly, especially in school districts that are commonly entrenched in a history of rules, bureaucracy, and regulations.
- Always meet with your children's teachers *first*! Nothing antagonizes a teacher more than being called in by the principal concerning a parent meeting that occurred without her. No one enjoys being blindsided—not the teacher, not you, not the administrator, not your children!

Also, a wonderful new book has just been published as a service publication of NAGC (The National Association for Gifted Children) through Prufrock Press Inc.: *Aiming for Excellence: Gifted Program*

Standards by Landrum, Callahan, and Shaklee (2001). It benchmarks standards of excellence in seven crucial areas:

- Program design
- Program administration and management
- Socioemotional guidance and counseling
- Student identification
- Curriculum and instruction
- Professional development
- Program evaluation

The authors provide an increased understanding of the current standards, providing examples, benefits, outcomes, and possible barriers to the successful implementation of the standards.

Access this book, read it carefully, and you'll feel and be much better equipped intellectually and emotionally as you approach your children's teachers and administrators.

Q. What is the best style of teacher for gifted children? Strict? Lax? One who requires a great deal of homework? Formal? Structured?

A. You should always expect your child's teacher to have high expectations for excellence, for your child and herself. Of course, this should be true for all children and teachers. Giving large amounts of homework is not a sign of good teaching. In fact, it's just the opposite. If a child already knows how to do the material, such as the current math problems, then doing more than four or five problems at home for review/reinforcement is a sad waste of your child's time. If a child isn't able to do the day's assignment, then sitting in front of a worksheet with thirty problems alone at home isn't going to do him any good, either.

Many times, schools select teachers for their gifted programs who are very dedicated, creative, and caring of their students. That's a start. However, in the last two decades, a multitude of research on teaching gifted and programming for gifted has surfaced. Courses and degrees are being offered at local college and universities in the specialty area of teaching the gifted. At this point, I believe it is not enough to be "well intentioned" as an educator of the gifted. Parents have the right to expect their gifted child's teacher to be credentialed in the topic and continuously undergoing staff development and studies in the area.

I ran a classroom with a great deal of flexibility. If students finished their work ahead of others, they had choices as to what they could do with their time while waiting—read, work on other assignments, do research in the library, work on computer programs, etc. They still had to check in with me before choosing. Sometimes I would say, "Fine, just clean and organize your desk first!"

You should also look for a teacher who integrates spelling and vocabulary lessons from all of the subject areas and special-area classes, rather than a premade publisher's spelling books. This makes the vocabulary studies much more applicable.

Differentiating the curriculum and compacting for gifted children make a huge difference in the quality use of their time and optimal learning.

There are teachers who support the rights of all children, including the gifted. Find them for your child—and find them to give them your support!

Q. Once my child has been identified as gifted and recommended for our district's gifted program, must I place Tonya in it? I've heard the homework load is overwhelming for the students who are in the gifted program.

A. I applaud your question and encourage you to talk with the teachers in the gifted program and visit the classrooms. Seeing and hearing what's going on firsthand is much better than getting information second- or thirdhand.

I taught the fourth-grade entrance class for the self-contained gifted program in a district for eighteen years. Parents were often initially overwhelmed at first, by hearing their children labeled as gifted and wondering what the "right" thing was to do for their children.

We would have an introductory evening where our program and philosophies would be explained and discussed. Dozens of questions would be asked and answered. By the end of the three hours, parents walked away with concrete answers based in fact, not gossip.

Having your child labeled as gifted does set him apart and doesn't always help. For that reason, I am now a strong proponent of an inclusive process rather than an exclusive program for gifted and all children!

Many parents of my gifted students over the years have become life-long friends of mine, as have their children. We're all advocating for the same thing: a quality education meeting the cognitive and affective needs of *all* children.

Q. I've had it! I've tried every possible way I know of to get our school district to educate our three children, each of whom has tested five to eight years above the norm in all areas of academic achievement. I even volunteered to help the teachers in the classrooms on a daily basis. The most that has happened is our seven-year-old daughter was given three times more work to do than her classmates were. The same has happened to our two sons! Can I gather support if I pursue the legal system?

A. I must admit, I secretly always hoped that a courageous family would turn to the legal system to help its cognitively gifted children get a fair and appropriate education once our school district had dropped its gifted and talented program. It would also have helped me help them!

There are three sources I would like you to familiarize yourself with before you undertake the legal system for support:

First, the *Jacob K. Javits Gifted and Talented Students Education Act of 1988, Part B*. Keep a copy of this with you, and memorize the Statement of Purpose (169):

> This act provides financial assistance to state and local agencies, institutions of higher education, and other public and private agencies and organizations, and initiates a coordinated program of research, demonstration projects, personnel training, and similar activities designed to build a nationwide capability in elementary and secondary schools to identify and meet the special educational needs of gifted and talented students. It is also the purpose of this act to supplement and make more effective the expenditure of state and local funds and of federal funds made available under chapter 2 of Title I and Title II of this act, for the education of gifted and talented students.

Simply stated, there have been, and continue to be, hundreds of thousands of dollars allocated to major colleges, universities, and school districts throughout our country since the inception of the Jacob K. Javits Gifted and Talented Students Education Act of 1988 for the research, demonstration, teacher training, and similar activities related to gifted education. Investigate your local districts to see what funds and programs or projects are available for your children and local educators.

Second is *Gifted Children and the Law: Mediation, Due Process, and Court Cases*, by F. Karnes and R. Marquardt, Ohio Psychology Press, 1991. This text is a valuable resource and major contribution in the advocacy of gifted education.

It provides the results of legal action and reinforcing a free and appropriate education for exceptional children (PL 94-142, The Education for All Handicapped Children Act). Parents can read about cases in which the courts clearly ruled in favor of parents and their gifted children.

Third is *Gifted Children and Legal Issues in Education: Parents' Stories of Hope*, by F. Karnes and R. Marquardt, Ohio Psychology Press, 1991.

This book is a wonderful resource for parents and teachers, as well as those who have become exhausted and exasperated in trying to ensure an appropriate education for their gifted and talented children and students.

Filled with a compilation of personal stories by parents of gifted children, this book lends support to parents by transmitting successfully settled disputes of parents whose determination and fortitude to achieve excellence in education for their own children and all children were victorious!

6

GIFTED CHILDREN SPEAK TO US

Gifted children talk about . . .

- Being gifted
- Children
- Parents
- Teachers
- School
- Thinking
- America
- A good teacher through the eyes of a gifted child

For years, every summer I ran a two-week cultural arts course for gifted nine- to thirteen-year-olds in our county. The children and I always had a wonderful time together. On the very last morning, I would take a peaceful hour with them—soft lights, easy music—and tell the story of Kahlil Gibran's *The Prophet*. I would then ask the children to honor me by being my prophet, answering some of the age-old questions of humankind.

I don't believe I ever underestimated the abilities of my students, but I never ceased to be awed by them.

Following are just a few of the hundreds of responses I received. I'm sure you'll enjoy them as much as the parents and I did.

SPEAK TO ME ABOUT BEING GIFTED ...

To me, it means something special, something unique. You don't need to get great grades or be very smart. You are gifted if you want to touch the sky, if you want to stretch the limit. If you follow your spirit, your heart, your mind, you are gifted. (Jessica, age 11)

Many people wonder what gifted means. It is my belief that it truly has no specific meaning. It may mean you are talented or smart, or maybe just proud of who you are. You can stretch the limits of this word and make it fit your spirit. (Kat, age 10)

Gifted means being blessed by God with something special. (Steven, age 12)

I think being gifted means having an IQ of 135 or more. (Frank, age 9)

A gifted student is a person who is above the clouds and cannot see the ground from where he started from, but can see his destination in the stars. (Carl, age 11)

SPEAK TO ME ABOUT CHILDREN ...

Children are like the seeds of the future to me. They are the people who will change the world tomorrow and they will succeed in doing so. They are different from adults in a way that they stretch their hands out to the stars and try new things. They are free at heart, mind, and spirit. (Jessica, age 11)

Children are young adults who have a lot to learn before they grow up. (Eric, age 10)

Children are little people that haven't learned everything about life. They also make more mistakes than adults. (Alex, age 10)

Children are all the members of a particular species that have a mother and father. (Steven, age 12)

Children are people who have very little responsibilities. They can run and play and learn every minute, every instant. They are the plaster, still sifting into the mold, not yet complete. (Molly, age 10)

A child is anybody who is eighteen years old or younger. (Frank, age 9)

Children are very mentally and physically fragile. (Andrew, age 11)

SPEAK TO ME ABOUT PARENTS ...

Parents are like the sun that nourishes the seed. They love and care for their children, watch them grow and watch them change the world. Parents bring life into the world and raise it. They are the leaders of their children who will be the leaders of theirs. They guide us through the hard times, the times when we don't have faith. (Jessica, age 11)

Parents guide us to our health, our faith, our life. They shape us to be who we are, teach us right from wrong. They are our mothers who brought us onto this earth and the fathers who teach us sports and how to be tough and not to give up. They are our leaders. (Kat, age 10)

Parents are people who try to do the best for their children. (Eric, age 10)

Parents are important people because they help children grow and learn so that they can take their rightful places in the world. Without parents, children wouldn't get the nurturing they need. (Jeffrey, age 11)

Parents are people who can help you when things seem hopeless. Children also reflect their parents. (Andrew, age 11)

Parents are people who shine light on the path of life, even though they cannot walk the whole journey with their children. (Carl, age 11)

Parents are people who gave you birth and boss you around. (Katie, age 9)

SPEAK TO ME ABOUT TEACHERS ...

Teachers are more than just people who tutor you in math, writing, history, etc. They teach you the precious things that will bond with you for as long as you live. Anyone is a teacher; parents, schoolteachers, friends, even children. They all help us grow joyously and well. Teachers are filled with love and care. They are friends to their students and all who know them. (Jessica, age 11)

Teachers are people who teach you and help you progress in life, if they are good ones, they will care how you're doing in school. (Andrew, age 11)

SPEAK TO ME ABOUT SCHOOL . . .

School is a building filled with learning. It overflows with children who reach to the sky and succeed. It's where friendship sprouts and people come together into one. When I think of a school, a ring of children holding hands and learning comes to mind. School is a building of courage, trying new things, friendship, and learning. (Jessica, age 11)

School is where people of all ages go to learn new things and be taught the skills that they need in the world. (Jeffrey, age 11)

School can change the lives of millions because it is the place where teachers teach, the children learn, and the cultural world grows. (Molly, age 10)

School is a place where children go to learn things to help them in life. Sometimes people who aren't very good in school don't like school and good students like it better. (Elise, age 11)

School is a place where learning is the key and being with friends is an especially fun part. (Aileen, age 9)

School is a place where average students learn. Gifted students learn anywhere else. (Carl, age 11)

SPEAK TO ME ABOUT THINKING . . .

Thinking is like a seedling that grows through the tangle of my mind. It keeps on flourishing, until it bursts from its shell onto a sheet of paper. Like a waterfall, it keeps on pouring. When a dream forms, I flow with it, wherever it may go. I can travel to the moon if I think about it. Thought is the beginning of a wonderful journey which can take you anywhere in the world. (Jessica, age 11)

Thinking—What is 2 + 2? If you answered, you were just thinking. (Kat, age 10)

Thinking is when you use your wits to figure out the answer to a problem. (Alex, age 10)

Thinking is when anyone in the world has a thought and studies it in their brain. It is how we come up with ideas that make the world better. (Jeffrey, age 11)

Thinking is what you do when you are trying to figure something out or trying to get an idea. (Julie, age 10)

Thinking is what you do all the time. You have to think about everything you do. You have to think about what question you want to ask me. (Ben, age 11)

AMERICA

By Carl Adair

My country tis' of thee . . .
Ringing bells of
freedom unite your
states of
being.
The vastness of your
beauty radiates
Strength and courage
within our
hearts.
Your many cultures
Races,
Religions,
Are a
Rainbow
Projected through
The prism of
Immigration,
Whose artists,
Musicians, and
Scientists,
Make up your nature.
Yet your honorable
Record is not without
Blemishes

Fractures litter your
Surface of bronze,
Paining with the
Violence
Our hates have created.
Americans of different
Color, race or thinking listen
To each other with
Misunderstanding.
Yet the magnificence of your
Freedom dwarfs this and
The other problems
That have survived and grown
Through the decades of striving
For excellence.
Too often your inhabitants
Take for granted the
Fact they have their own
One among many others.
These tones, when played
Together, not only ring true in perfect
Harmony,
But the awesome chorus of our
American Society.
. . . Sweet land of liberty
Of thee I sing.

A GOOD TEACHER THROUGH THE EYES OF A GIFTED CHILD

By E'Shantee R. Proctor

Acknowledges my uniqueness.
Grants me the opportunities to creatively problem solve.
Opposed to the notion that I must be globally gifted.
Offers enriching opportunities and chances for real-life experiences.
Develops ways for me to learn at my level and pace.

Truly dedicated to my classmates and me.
Eases the tensions with a warm, loving, learning environment.
Appropriately differentiates the curriculum.
Convinced that I don't need to be separated from my peers.
Helps me reach the synthesis level of thinking.
Encourages me to be my best.
Realizes what works for me can work for all of my classmates.

ADDITIONAL RESOURCES

PROFESSIONAL ASSOCIATIONS AND ADVOCACY GROUPS FOR GIFTED EDUCATION

American Association for Gifted Children
Talented Identification Program
Duke University
1121 West Main Street, Suite 100
Durham, NC 27701
(919) 683-1400

American Mensa, Ltd.
2626 East 14th Street
Brooklyn, NY 11235

Association for the Gifted Council for Exceptional Children
1920 Association Drive
Reston, VA 22091
(800) 336-3278

The Council of State Directors of Programs for Gifted
G/T Programs Consultant
Maine Department of Education and Cultural Services
State House Station #23
Augusta, ME 04333

The Institute for Law and Gifted Education
909 South 34th Avenue
Hattiesburg, MS 39402

National Association for Creative Children and Adults
8080 Springvalley Drive
Cincinnati, OH 43236
(513) 631-1777

National Association for Gifted Children
1155 15th Street, N.W.
Suite 1002
Washington, DC 20005
(202) 785-4268

National Association of State Boards of Education
526 Hall of the States
444 North Capital Street, N.W.
Washington, DC 20001
(202) 624-5845

Supporting Emotional Needs of the Gifted
School of Professional Psychology
Wright State University
P.O. Box 2745
Dayton, OH 45435

World Council for Gifted and Talented Children, Inc.
Executive Secretary
College of Education
Leman University
Beaumont, TX 77704

JOURNALS FOR GIFTED EDUCATION

Gifted Child Quarterly
1155 15th Street, N.W., Suite 1002
Washington, DC 20005
(202) 785-9268

Gifted Child Today
P.O. Box 8813
Waco, TX 76714
(800) 998-2208

Journal for the Education of the Gifted
University of North Carolina Press
P.O. Box 2288
Chapel Hill, NC 27515-2288

Journal for the Education of the Gifted (JEG)
1920 Association Drive
Reston, VA 22091

Mensa Research Journal
19340 Dunbridge Way
Gaithersburg, MD 20879

Roeper Review
Roeper City and County Schools
P.O. Box 329
Bloomfield Hills, MI 48303-0329
(313) 642-1500

INTERNET SITES

EPGY – Education Program for Gifted Youth
http://Kanpai.stanford.edu/epgy/

ERIC Clearinghouse for Exceptional Children
www.aspensys.com/eric/index.html

Family Education Network
http://familyeducation.com/email/

The Gifted Child Society
www.gifted.org/

The Gifted and Talented (TAG) Resources Home Page
www.eskimo.com/~user/kids.html

Institute for the Academic Advancement of Youth Center for Talented Youth
www.jhu.edu:80/~gifted/

National Resource Center on the Gifted and Talented (NCR/GT)
www.ucc.ucon.edu:80/~wwwgt/

The Tag Family Network
www.telport.com/~rKaltwas/tag/

Yahoo Resources for Gifted Youth K-12
www.yahoo.com/text/education/K_12/Gifted_Youth

BIBLIOGRAPHY

Adderholdt, M., and J. Goldberg. 1999. *Perfectionism: What's Bad about Being Too Good?* Minneapolis, Minn.: Free Spirit Press.

Bloom, B., ed. 1984. *Taxonomy of Educational Objectives: Handbook of the Cognitive Domain.* New York: Longmans, Green.

Callahan, C., and C. A. Tomlinson. 1996. *Heterogeneity: Inclusion or Delusion? Can We Make Academically Diverse Classrooms Succeed?* Alexandria, Va.: Association for Supervision and Curriculum Development.

Chall, J. S., and S. S. Conrad. 1991. *Should Textbooks Challenge Students? The Case for Easier or Harder Textbooks.* New York: Teachers College Press.

Cimochowski, A. 1993. *Cloze In on Social Studies.* New York: Berrent Publications.

Coleman, R., and J. Gallagher. 1995. "Appropriate Differentiated Services: Guides for Best Practices in the Education of Gifted Children." *Gifted Child Today Magazine* 18, no. 5: 32–33.

Conrad, S., and D. Flegler. 1993. *Math Contest: Grade 7 and 8 and Algebra Course 1.* Tenafly, N.J.: Math League Press.

Cymerman, S., and D. Modest. 1984. *SAGE: The Spice of Learning for Gifted and Talented.* Longmont, Colo.: Sopris West.

Erickson, H. 1998. *Concept-based Curriculum and Instruction: Teaching beyond the Facts.* Thousand Oaks, Calif.: Corwin Press.

Flanders, J. R. 1987. "How Much of the Content in Mathematics Textbooks Is New?" *Arithmetic Teacher* 35, no 1: 18–23.

Galbraith, J. 1983. *The Gifted Kids, Survival Guide for Ages 11–18*. Minneapolis, Minn.: Free Spirit Press.

Galbraith, J., and J. Delisle. 1996. *The Gifted Kids' Survival Guide: A Teen Handbook*. Minneapolis, Minn.: Free Spirit Press.

Gallagher, J., and S. Gallagher. 1994. *Teaching the Gifted Child*. 4th ed. Boston: Allyn and Bacon.

Gardner, H. 1993. *Multiple Intelligences: The Theory in Practice*. New York: Basic Books.

———. 1984. *Frames of Mind: The Theory of Multiple Intelligences*. New York: Basic Books.

Hipp, E. 1995. *Fighting Invisible Tigers*. Minneapolis, Minn.: Free Spirit Press.

Karnes, F., and R. Marquardt, eds. 1991. *Gifted Children and Legal Issues in Education*. Dayton: Ohio Psychology Press.

———. 1991. *Gifted Children and the Law*. Dayton: Ohio Psychology Press.

Kerr, B. A. 1991. *A Handbook for Counseling the Gifted and Talented*. Alexandria, Va.: American Counseling Association.

———. 1997. *Smart Girls: A New Psychology of Girls, Women, and Giftedness*. Scottsdale, Ariz.: Gifted Psychology Press.

Kerr, B., and S. Cohn. 2001. *Smart Boys: Talent, Manhood, and the Search for Meaning*. Scottsdale, Ariz.: Gifted Psychology Press.

Khatena, J. 1982. *Educational Psychology of the Gifted*. New York: Wiley.

Landrum, M., C. Callahan, and B. Shaklee. 2001. *Aiming for Excellence: Gifted Program Standards*. Waco, Tex.: Prufrock Press.

Reis, S. M. 1994. "How Schools Are Shortchanging the Gifted." *Technology Review* 97, no. 3: 38–45.

———. 1995. "Providing Equity for All: Meeting the Needs of High Ability Students." In *Beyond Tracking: Finding Success in Inclusive Schools*, ed. H. Dod and J. A. Page, 119–131. Bloomington, Ind.: Phi Delta Kappa.

Reis, S. M., D. E. Burns, and J. S. Renzulli. 1992. *Curriculum Compacting: The Complete Guide to Modifying the Regular Curriculum for High-Ability Students*. Mansfield Center, Conn.: Creative Learning Press.

Reis, S. M., J. Westberg, J. Kulikowich, F. Caillard, T. Hebert, J. H. Purcell, J. Rogers, J. Swist, and J. Plucker. 1992. *An Analysis of Curriculum Compacting on Classroom Practices: Technical Report*. Storrs, Conn.: National Research Center on the Gifted and Talented.

Robinson, A. 1990. "Point-Counterpoint: Cooperation or Exploitation? The Argument against Cooperative Learning for Talented Students." *Journal for the Education of the Gifted* 14: 9–27.

Ross, P., ed. 1993. *National Excellence: A Case for Developing America's Talent*. Washington, D.C.: U.S. Department of Education.

Schwartz, L. L. 1994. "Educating the Gifted to the Gifted: A National Resource." In *Why Give "Gifts" to the Gifted: Investing in a National Resource,*
1–7. Thousands Oaks, Calif.: Corwin Press.

Sternberg, R. 1997. "What Does It Mean to Be Smart?" *Educational Leadership* 546: 20–24.

Terman, L. M. 1947. *Mental and Physical Traits of a Thousand Gifted Children: Genetic Studies of Genius.* Vol. 1. Stanford, Calif.: Stanford University
Press.

Tomlinson, C. 1999. *The Differentiated Classroom: Responding to the Needs of
All Learners.* Alexandria Va.: Association for Supervision and Curriculum
Development.

Treffinger, D. J., C. Callahan, and V. L. Baughn. 1991. "Research on Enrichment Efforts in Gifted Education." In *Handbook of Special Education: Research and Practice.* Vol. 4: *Emerging Programs,* ed. M. C. Wang, M. C.
Reynolds, and H. J. Walberg, 37–55. Oxford: Pergamon Press.

Usiskin, Z. 1987. "Why Elementary Algebra Can, Should, and Must Be an
Eighth-Grade Course for Average Students." *Mathematics Teacher* 80, no. 6:
428–38.

Webb, J. T. 1982. *Guiding the Gifted Child.* Columbus: Ohio Psychology Publishing Company

Winebrenner, S. 1992. *Teaching Gifted Kids in the Regular Classroom.* Minneapolis, Minn.: Free Spirit Press.

Winner, E. 1996. *Gifted Children.* New York: Basic Books.

INDEX

4-MAT, 23

abstract random, 10
Accelerated Reader (AR), 23
acceleration, 13
Adair, Carl, 85
advanced placement (AP) courses, 13, 22, 46
advocacy, 71, 74; information gathering, 75
America's Genius, 56
anti-social behavior, 41–42

books: for gifted teens, 33–35; for parents, 4; list of Caldecott Medal winners, 28–30; list of favorite children's books, 36–38; list of Newbery Medal winners, 26–27; on perfectionism, 51; with gifted characters, 30
burnout, 43, 50

Caldecott, Randolph, 28
Caldecott books: list of medal winners, 28–30
Chambellan, René Paul, 24
common sense, 9–10
consultant teachers, 12
counseling, 41–43, 48
curriculum compacting, 12, 16–17, 54
curriculum differentiation, 11, 17–19

depression, 48–49
differentiation, *see* curriculum differentiation

enrichment, 11, 20–21

feelings, 6

Gardner, Howard, 1
goals, setting of, 8

ABOUT THE AUTHOR

Dr. Rosemary Callard-Szulgit is currently associated with the State University of New York, Brockport, where her courses on teaching the gifted have become highly respected. She is also CEO of her own staff development consulting and business and the former facilitator for gifted and talented, K–8 in the Webster Central School District in Rochester, New York. Her education consulting business, Partners for Excellence, is located in both Rochester, New York, and Phoenix, Arizona.

Callard-Szulgit's initial training and teaching focus with gifted education has expanded into districtwide integrated programs servicing all children. Her interest and focus on educating children at their aptitudinal levels has succeeded through the combinations of curriculum compacting and differentiation coupled with acceleration.

Recognized in *Who's Who among American Educators*, Rosemary brings thirty-four years of research and classroom experience in elementary, middle school, and university settings to her role as staff development trainer of parents, teachers, and children throughout the country.

She has spoken at the First United States/China Conference on Education, Beijing, and presented for the American Creativity Association,

National Association for Gifted, World Council on Gifted, West Virginia
Annual Reading Conference, and the United States/Russia Conference
on Education, as well as consulting throughout the United States. She
continues to have articles published dealing with the education of gifted
children.